Also from **Cat's-paw Press**

Roughing It Elegantly:
A Practical Guide to Canoe Camping

The Paddler's Planner

The Prepublishing Handbook

What you should know
***before* you publish your first book**

by
Patricia J. Bell

Foreword
by
Dan Poynter

Eden Prairie, Minnesota

The **Prepublishing Handbook —** What You Should Know Before You Publish Your First Book

 For information address Cat's-paw Press, 9561 Woodridge Circle, Eden Prairie, Minnesota 55347.

Printed in the United States of America
97 96 95 94 93 10 9 8 7 6 5 4 3 2 1

Book cover design: Patrick M. Redmond
Patrick Redmond Design, St. Paul, Minnesota
Photo credits: Daniels Photography

Library of Congress Cataloging in Publication Data

Bell, Patricia J., 1931-
The **Prepublishing Handbook.**

Includes reading recommendations and index.

1. Publishing
2. Self-publishing
3. Desktop publishing
4. Entrepreneurship
5. Little presses
6. Self-publishing—Hand books, manuals, etc.

Z285.5B 1992 070.5 92-72686
ISBN 0-9618227-2-4

Contents

Foreword

The *Prepublishing Handbook: What you should know* before *you publish your first book* is the book to read if you consider self-publishing. In a friendly, conversational manner, Pat Bell gives a thorough overview of what lies ahead for prospective self-publisher—the peaks, the valleys, the traps, the rewards. She gives a clear picture of what beginning publishers get themselves into.

The *Prepublishing Handbook* urges the new author to evaluate the chances for successful publication of the manuscript among the flood of new books appearing each year. She also explores definitions of "successful publication."

Aside from the desire to publish a book, the basic issue is Do I have the time and the money to invest in the project? The financial costs alone are substantial. Speaking from her own experience as a self-publisher, Pat frankly lays out the numbers for expenses that can be expected.

The more you work on a book's promotion, the more likely it is to succeed. This means you spend a lot of time. Book sales entail work. As the staff of one in your publishing house, you perform a great many different tasks calling for different personality traits and skills. Pat Bell examines these various roles and asks, Do you have the temperament *and* the time to perform all these jobs effectively?

Pat was a teacher. It shows in her demonstration that self-education can overcome many obstacles. She identifies the copious resources available from libraries, booksellers and people. She stresses the value of publishers' organizations for their exchanges of information and experience.

You learn by doing. It saves effort to have some idea of what you need to learn and why you need to learn it. Throughout The *Prepublishing Handbook,* the attitude is "Publishing your book can be done; you *can* do it, and you can do it better, knowing ahead what needs to be done and preparing yourself to do it."

Dan Poynter
Author-Publisher
The Self-Publishing Manual

Acknowledgments

Thank goodness I didn't have to be The Little Red Hen on this book. I asked for help while writing it, and the many people who helped me develop and produce this book made it a better book. I am truly fortunate, and I am most grateful to them. First thanks go to those people who took my Pitfalls of Publishing class. This is where this book started.

In this book, I speak of the value of using "Friendly Readers" to seek out weak spots, goofs and strengths in a manuscript. The finished result is testimony to the importance of such advice. I am deeply indebted to numerous Friendly Readers at various stages in the development of the manuscript.

Specific and special thanks to the following for reading the first draft and their comments: Dr. Constance Sansome (Trailblazer Books); Cindy Reever (Aris Publishing); Herb Weyrauch (Beebe Books), Darryl A. Zurn and Maridee Ennis. Their remarks led to major shifts in the arrangement of material. Cindy also has come to the rescue when I have had computer problems.

Readers of the second version included Pati Gelfman (Resources Publication Group) and Connie Babcock (who provided some very helpful insights), among others.

Marlin and Loris Bree of MarLor Press offered useful points from their experience in the publishing world. Loris has been a much valued source of aid and comfort throughout—friend to talk to, generous sharer of experience, friendly reader and focus group participant. Both are generous with encouragement.

Thanks too go to Karen Searle (Dos Tejedoras Fiber Arts Publications), Laura Zahn (Down to Earth Publications), and Eileen Cavanaugh (Hennepin County Library) for their much-valued comments. They are all very special people, and dear to me.

The Midwest Independent Publishers Association deserves mention, too. In its community, and it truly *is* a community, I have found valued friends and colleagues, many of whom gave specific help. I should not omit, either, the encouragement and support from others farther out from my ring of activity.

This is also a good place to salute Mary Birmingham, the director of METRONET, the metropolitan library network serving the Minneapolis-St. Paul-metropolitan county area. This extraordinary lady is a kindred spirit in the matter of developing networks and collecting information.

A phone call one day from Nancy Gronbeck led to the section on electronic databases, an area I had been only dimly aware of. Her comments and suggestions should open up several avenues of information for readers and writers.

A good editor makes a writer's work shine. Rosemary Wallner was a wonderful editor to work with. She too suggested additions that enhance the book.

Theresa Wolner and Eileen Quam indexed this work, demonstrating the value of professional work, and Pat Ricci attended to the Cataloging in Publication. Their work is *much* appreciated.

Patrick M. Redmond (Patrick Redmond Design) not only designed the cover for this book, but was also tremendously helpful in pointers on marketing and design and full of useful ideas. Working with him was an illuminating experience and great fun.

Finally, I am most grateful to Dan Poynter for his kindness in writing a foreword to this book. I originally ventured into the publishing world following the directions he so clearly lays out in *The Self-Publishing Manual*, an invaluable resource for any who decide to publish independently.

Throughout all the entire project of developing and producing this book, I have had the continuing love, encouragement and support from my husband Don. He is the base that makes the whole thing possible.

Patricia J. Bell

Introduction

All kinds of people write their first books for all kinds of reasons and with all kinds of subject matter. Many naively think that getting it published is a sure thing, that publishers are eagerly awaiting their manuscript, and that their book will sell like mad. In the search for publication, many learn of the four options: find a publisher; go to a vanity press, publish it independently, or drop the dream. The second option is not a good choice; the fourth one is taken reluctantly. Which leaves the matter at finding a publisher or doing it oneself.

I have been in those shoes. I spent several fruitless years searching for a publisher for my first book and only accidentally learned about the possibility of independent publication. I was very fortunate, too, in that by living in the Minneapolis-Saint Paul metropolitan area, I could link with others who had published their own work.

In associating with other independent publishers, I realized a common bond was that most of us really did not know what we were getting ourselves into when we began. We who sort of wandered into publishing might not have done so if we had known what we eventually learned.

With this realization, I began teaching classes that looked at what was demanded by publication. In the class, we looked at the education or training needed to perform the various functions of a single-person publishing house (is this a publishing room?). We considered the amount of time involved in performing the numerous tasks. We laid out expenditures—obvious and not so apparent—in producing and promoting a book and running the business. We looked at why books are or are not published, and a book's chances of succeeding. We perceived that personal temperament is an important factor, too.

The purpose of the class (called Pitfalls of Publishing: do you *really* want to publish your own book?) then was to give people thinking about publishing a book some background, from which they could make an informed decision before proceeding. This book grew out of those sessions. The *Prepublishing Handbook* is a whether-to, not a how-to book. Now, as then, the purpose is to equip an author with knowledge of what it takes to publish and promote a book. It offers more beyond a warning about the risks and costs, though. It is important for a person contemplating self-publication to know that enormous resources exist, and many are identified in the Recommended Reading and Information Resources sections. *Using* those resources also will help the prospective publisher make a better book and promote it more successfully.

I suspect that I am an example of a typical first-book publisher. I had a book that I thought was useful. I was willing to do all the work necessary and I was able to do much of it. My company remains small. While often a first-book publisher goes on, producing more titles and growing, many will not. This book is truly a book for the would-be beginner.

Independently publishing my first book taught me many things, and I have found the education is a continuing process. It led me along in directions I had not considered. In short, it changed much of my life. I have worked happily at being a publisher. There are some splendid people in the small press community, and my life has been greatly enriched by knowing and working with them. But that is *my* experience. It gives no guarantee to someone else. Publishing is not everybody's cup of tea, and that's fine. The trick is in finding out ahead of time if it is not yours.

So. I hope this book will help *you* determine whether you want to publish a book. If the answer is yes, then go for it. Set your goals, what you expect in personal development as well as business development. With reasonable expectations, the project can be a rewarding experience on many levels. If the answer is no, that's fine, too. Put your energies and money to better advantage for you. A thorough awareness and appreciation of one's abilities, capacities and interests is valuable. The key point is that the decision should be the right one for you.

Whichever way you go, I wish you all the best.

1

Why Does Anyone Publish?

THERE it is, pages and pages of manuscript. What a wonderful title page, with your name in plain view! You have poured yourself in to the writing. You have dreamed of seeing it finished, and there it is! Now, can your manuscript become a *real* book, a published book? It is merely a dream or can a dream come true? Can you make your dream happen? Who publishes books? For that matter, why is any book published?

Books are published for various reasons. Equally diverse are the publishers.

One group of publishers comprises companies whose business is publishing books. Such companies, or publishing houses, are interested in making money. They tend to produce books that will sell in huge quantities. Some develop specialty areas, garnering reputations as literary houses. Other organizations or special interest groups may publish informational books focusing on their particular area of interest.

Some people—or more particularly, companies or organizations—publish specialized material for a relatively narrow audience. Companies publish or produce training manuals, or instructional material to accompany products such as computer software. Foundations or special interest groups, such as the Arthritis Foundation, may aim at providing information to a particular group. They may not be overly interested in the marketing aspects of publishing. Charitable organizations publish to provide a product for fund-raising—cookbooks are a common product for this purpose.

Some people or companies publish because they acquire information which they believe is of value to others. Though these books, such as the directories (several of which are listed in Information Resources), may not be particularly exciting, they are useful. Some are specialized to greater or lesser extent, and would be of concern to particular segments of the population only. Some are highly technical or arcane.

Business purposes are not always the prime mover for publishing a book. Individuals or small groups may decide to publish a family history, or a history of a company, city or area. Often, these books are usually private printings of a limited number of copies and may not be intended for the marketplace, even though many of the same decisions (such as how to get a nice finished product that wouldn't break the family bank) that must be made for a commercial publication apply to a private publication. If this is your reason for publishing, much of this book still applies, with the exception of the emphasis on marketing.

Some authors choose to publish their work themselves because that is the only way they have to get their particular viewpoint or set of information to a desired larger audience. Often, other people consider these author/publishers "ax-grinders." True, seeing one's name on a book provides a great deal of gratification.

On a few occasions, authors may decide to publish their own work because they can get their book into print faster than a larger publishing house. This is why in 1983 Richard Nixon independently published *Real Peace.* Independent publishing happens, too, when events are breaking rapidly, and an early book has a better chance to capture a spot on the market. On December 13, 1990, Col. Trevor Dupuy, USA Ret., testified before Congress on what to expect if war should erupt in the Persian Gulf. He thought a paperback book on the subject would be timely. The co-publisher of his two earlier books agreed and approached paperback publishers regarding the project. The reaction was uniformly negative, with the argument that if war did come, it would be over before the book could come out. Dupuy decided to publish *If War Comes...How to Defeat Saddam Hussein* himself (Hero Books). He ordered 1,000 copies in trade paperback format. As eager buyers snapped up the copies, Depuy placed a second order for 2,500.

With the actual start of war in January, 1991, interest became even keener. Dupuy sold United Kingdom rights to a specialist in military publishing. He was invited to appear on every U.S. television network and on the BBC and *The Wall Street Journal* ran a story about *If War Comes.*

The upshot of all the interest was that Warner Books reconsidered its earlier position. Negotiations followed, with Dupuy getting a $25,000 advance for mass market rights. Warner's edition of *If War Comes* was rushed to press as *How to Defeat Iraq: Scenarios and*

Strategies for the Gulf War. The company ordered a run of 600,000 copies and shipped to stores in mid-February, 1991.

The majority of people who publish their own books, however, do so because they were unable to find books on an area of particular interest. Self-help books on a huge range of topics result.

What Are Your Options?

Almost everyone at some time has said, "I could write a book!" Some do—and in the United States, more than 47,000 were published in 1991, on an astonishing range of topics. What are your options for making *your* dream a reality?

Find A Publisher

Once you decide to publish, your first option is find a publisher. They are out there—more than 10,000 of them, though many publish only one or two books. Some 5,000 new publishers appear each year, while similar numbers cease publication or merge into other publishing companies. To get some notion of how many publishers there are, go to your local library. Look into *Books in Print* (referred to as *BIP*), which lists all the books in print by author, title and publisher. The author listings alone appear in three volumes—each large enough to give a small child a boost at the dinner table. Check the annual *Literary Market Place* or *Writer's Market.* Either will give you an idea of how many publishers are interested in acquiring manuscripts for publication.

Then identify the publishers whose books are related in some respects to your manuscript. Find the appropriate editorial focus. Clearly, it is pointless to submit a poetry manuscript to a publisher who produces auto repair manuals. *Literary Market Place* now has a subsection entitled "Small Press Publishers" which details areas of specialization, unique publications or first-time ventures. Keep in mind that small presses may not accept manuscripts. If you do decide to publish your book, the experience will give you a much keener appreciation of why publishers reject manuscripts.

If you find a publisher, be sure you know how to present your project most favorably. Judith Appelbaum's or Richard Balkin's books on getting published (see Recommended Reading—Publishing) each give invaluable advice.

Make sure you send your manuscript to *legitimate* publishing houses. Beware of ads that invite authors to submit manuscripts for publication. Often these houses are the "vanity presses," though you may be sure they don't refer to themselves as such. The author pays the vanity press to publish his or her book. Presumably, the vanity press prepares the manuscript for production, sees it through production, tends to all the details of publication and promotes it. All too often, however, the author winds up with only a few precious (at a cost of thousands of dollars) copies and *nothing* happens in the book world. Horror stories about vanity presses abound. Instances of authors paying $10,000 and receiving only one or two copies of their books unfortunately are not rare. It is well understood in the publishing world that libraries and bookstores almost universally will not bother to buy books produced by a vanity press.

Or Publish Your Manuscript Yourself

The alternative option is to publish your manuscript yourself. In and of itself, do-it-yourself is not "vanity" publication, though originally the nature of books self-published often tended to create that impression. Self-publication, or to use the preferred term, independent publication, is the Little Red Hen approach. You remember her story—when she asked for help, nobody was willing to help her plant her grain, tend it, harvest it, grind it or make the bread. "Not I, not I," everyone said. But when baked bread time came ("Who will eat my bread?"), she gave the hungry moochers the same answer that she had had to give herself: "Very well then, I'll do it myself." The self-publisher, or independent publisher, is an entrepreneur. He or she uses his or her own money to produce the product. In the long run, people who have carefully educated themselves in the matter of publishing and who shop carefully can get far more for the publishing dollar by publishing it independently than by having a vanity press produce the book.

Is book publishing a terribly arcane matter calling for all sorts of specialized information? Does it require that the individual know important people in all sorts of places? Does that person have to be far above average in intelligence? Not necessarily. However, it takes lots of CPR—Courage, Persistence and Resourcefulness.

Several other attributes are important, not the least of which is a fairly substantial amount of cash. Independent publishing also takes a huge amount of time—not just the writing and publishing of the book—that's the easy part, but also insuring that boxes and boxes of the same book do not remain in your garage or basement. That's what this book is about. It will give you some notion of how much time and how much money you may be investing in the publication of your book.

The odds are formidable. Of the more than 47,000 books published in 1991, not all should have been published, and many will not remain in print long. Books go out of print at a rate of roughly 3,000 titles a year. The average life expectancy of a nonfiction book is about 43 months. Some, such as annual travel guides or computer books, have a life limited by time or rapidly moving technology. A novel's shelf life is generally a couple of months, less for a mass market book. Of those that remain, some go either to what is called the midlist or to the backlist (see Glossary), and many take up more or less permanent residence there. One would of course expect to be able to buy a copy of *Hamlet* at any bookstore. Backlist titles such as *Hamlet* become staples, like flour or sugar, no longer the object of much promotion, but still of value to the publisher and the book buyer. Some titles reach best-seller status simply by being durable backlist or midlist items that sell steadily year after year.

A randomly-selected issue of *Publishers Weekly*, the news magazine of the book trade, listed 106 titles declared out of print. (Books are declared out of print generally when the publisher has run out of stock of the title.) Included were 23 specialized annuals. In fact, a company (UMI) specializing in out-of-print titles claims to have 114,000 titles.

What Are Your Expectations?

What do you want to achieve from the publication of your book? This is an important question that should be considered carefully before embarking on the venture of self-publication. If it is because you hope to make a major change in the world, you should know that you face enormous difficulties in merely getting the public, or an influential part of it, to be aware of your book and read it.

If you expect to get rich from the publication of your Great American Novel, or the trade paper wonder of the year, you had better have very modest definitions of *rich* or you will most likely be doomed to disappointment. Typically, an author receives as royalties 10 percent or less of the *publisher's sale* price of the book. (Some simple arithmetic here: If the book retails for $9.95, the publisher often gets only $4, which results in $0.40 per copy for our author.) Too, you must be prepared to spend an enormous amount of time over a lengthy period, and you should not expect to be compensated for more than a fraction of the time.

With publication and vigorous promotion of your book, you may find that you are getting some attention as an expert—after all, you wrote a book! Depending on the level of the expertise involved, you may find yourself speaking or writing or answering questions on your subject with much greater frequency.

If you believe that you have something definitely worthwhile to say, or information that people would value, and you believe enough in your book to invest your time and money in its publication, self-publication is a great adventure. You will find you must learn about things you never knew even existed but are now important to your project. Fields previously unknown to you will open up, and you will meet all sorts of interesting people along the way. You will find that your book takes on a life of its own, separate and distinct from what it was when it was still your manuscript.

Then, too, some of the consequences will be totally unexpected. You may find that promotional activities may lead you into avenues you had not previously considered. I published *Roughing It Elegantly: A Practical Guide to Canoe Camping* in 1987. At that time I never dreamed that I would someday write a book about publishing. Do you think Salmon Rushdie had any conception of the furor his *Satanic Verses* would create?

The objection of a larger publisher to many books is that the book's audience is limited, specialized or regional. Yet many small press books have done quite well *because* they were limited or specialized or regional. A major publisher has to sell 15,000 copies of a book just to break even. But a small publisher can make a profit on as few as 2,000 copies, since the small publisher has a much lower overhead. (We're not talking about the relatively few highly-touted titles from well-known authors, where the author receives five- or six-digit advances and huge promotional budgets are allotted. Publicity about those numbers hides the fact that such arrangements are exceptional rather than the rule.)

But before you decide to publish your own book(s), let's take a closer look at what is involved, and consider what you would be getting yourself into. Read on.

2

Should You Publish Your Own Book?

IF you decide to publish your own book, you will be in good company. There is a long and honorable tradition of backing up one's ideas and beliefs in writing with one's own financial resources. You would be joining the likes of Benjamin Franklin (as a printer, he had a running start), Henry Thoreau, Thomas Paine, William Blake, Washington Irving, Walt Whitman, and Mark Twain. A recent best-seller, self-published, (more than 23 weeks on the best-seller list in 1991) was *50 Simple Things You Can Do to Save the Earth*, an excellent example of a timely topic (environmentalism). (The publisher, the Earthworks Group/Earthworks Press, followed that one up with *50 Simple Things Kids Can Do to Save the Earth*). Other examples are John Muir's *How To Keep Your Volkswagen Alive*, Ken Blanchard's *One Minute Manager* and Dan Poynter's *Self-Publishing Manual*, all having become durable, long-selling titles, John Louis Anderson's *Scandinavian Humor and Other Myths*, Pat Dorff's *File, Don't Pile*™ and William Hull's ***All Hell Broke Loose.*** Blanchard's and Anderson's books were later published by major publishing houses.

If you believe your book has sufficient appeal, value or usefulness, and that belief is backed by some reader research, then you should also know that often those qualities can be more successfully exploited by a small publisher than by a larger one. One good case in point: Sybil Smith (Fins Publications) publishes fishing books about specific Minnesota areas, currently the metropolitan Minneapolis-Saint Paul lakes and the Brainerd-Whitefish area. Fishing is a popular activity and fishermen are always eager to know where and how to catch lots of the big ones. She can more efficiently and effectively exploit the market than can a large, New York-based company. Another author who has carved out a specialty niche is Laura Zahn. She began with books on historic Bed and Breakfast establishments in Minnesota and Wisconsin. She found that cookbooks derived from her research sold well and now has a series of them. The self-publisher can successfully publish a book that a larger publisher cannot if (and this is a huge if) the self-publisher can do most of the various tasks personally. Be warned that the pay is low at this point.

Literally thousands of small publishing companies are scattered throughout the country. Curiously, they are not all focused on nonfiction material. In an article on small presses (TWA *Ambassador*, October 1990, "Small Presses Flex Big Muscles," by Chauncey Mabe), Len Fulton of Dustbooks noted that it is the small publishing companies who meet the need for literary fiction, poetry, special-interest books and classics that otherwise would fall out of print—the sorts of subjects less interesting to major publishers. But these small houses are also meeting regional interests. "There is no question that most of the invention in the industry takes place at small presses. Every new problem gives a spurt to the small publishing companies. They are tackling new subjects and finding new ways to make books—and even new ways to market them," Fulton said.

Big houses are now run more with eye to bottom line—small houses go more for finding and developing talent, much as Alfred A. Knopf, Inc., used to do. Independent, small publishers have two major advantages. One is low overhead, primarily in fewer pay checks to cover. The other is the ability to respond quickly to shifts in public interests and tastes.

Do You Have What It Takes?

To make it as a publisher, you need four interior assets (personal characteristics) and one exterior asset.

You need to be creative. Of the many people who say they could write a book, only a few actually do it. The fact that you have a manuscript demonstrates some creativity. You will have to draw continually on that asset to get the manuscript into the form of an actual volume. You will have to be creative—resourceful—in composing promotional materials, in eliciting publicity, in devising and implementing strategies to get the book out into the wider world.

You need confidence. Remember that a book must be viewed as a product. A strong belief in the value of the product is tremendously important. You have to shift your attitude about the book. From being an intimate part of you—the author's being, your creation, your *baby*— the book will change into a product, a marketable item that will appeal to a particular segment of the public. This change in attitude is absolutely necessary. Once the book has taken tangible form, you the author must become as objective about it as is possible. Ideally, this objectivity will translate into a strong belief in the product. If sufficient research was done early enough in the manuscript's development and that research translated into solid material, then you should have the necessary confidence in the book to engage in itsvigorous promotion.

You also need confidence in yourself. You need to have a strong belief in yourself and your capabilities to do what has to be done. This need not be a major problem. If you were smart enough to write a good book, then you are smart enough to publish it. Remember, you can remedy ignorance through vigorous self-education. If you feel that ignorance prevails in too many of the areas to be entered, squelch that feeling by educating yourself. It does not take tremendous intelligence to produce a book. (No more than it seems to take to write one. One of 1990's best-sellers was purportedly written by Mildred Kerr Bush—White House First Dog Milly!) Continuing and careful study, developing a network of people who can be called on for advice, and some continuing successes, even if small, can all develop confidence.

A third asset is courage. Some might call it nerve, even rashness. A certain amount of risk arises when a person undertakes any sort of new project. The degree of risk depends on just how far the venture is expected to go, how much the unknown looms, the extent of preparations made to meet the risk, and the consequences of failure.

You see then the series of mental assets. You must be creative. That has been at least partially demonstrated. You need to be confident. That is demonstrated by thoroughly pursuing the question of publication In addition, you have confidence based on information. Having gotten past the points of creativity and confidence, assess your degree of courage. You must be willing to take the risks to venture into this project.

The fourth asset is stamina. Some might call it persistence. Whatever you call it, the trait is a vital ingredient in any entrepreneur's personal makeup. The determination to carry through is tremendously important now. Equally important is the *willingness* to persist, to follow through and to follow up. You will need much energy—physical, mental and emotional—to keep on doing what has to be done. You will at times be doing several things at once, and sometimes at a fairly rapid pace. You will need a great deal of mental energy to deal creatively with production and promotion plans for your book. You should plan how to maintain the energy level needed to persist. To maintain a satisfactory level of emotional energy, devise some strategies for stress relief. A regular program of physical exercise is helpful. Try also to include an activity in your life that is quite different—one that demands full attention for short periods of time. Fishing works well, as does gardening.

Finally, the all-important exterior asset is money. To publish a book is rather like buying a car, especially in the financial outlay. You decide on the size (how many copies), whether it will be the deluxe or the economy model, what extras it will have. Unlike buying a car, paying for publication will be virtually all up-front money. Set your priorities accordingly.

Your financial resources will be your own, primarily. Banks are not particularly interested in lending money on an untried, almost nebulous item such as a book or new publishing company. Expect that you will need at least $12,000 for the first year, and that immediate cash flow will be a problem. If you have done your work well, you may be able to generate income before the first year is out. It is possible to generate cash flow before the book is even printed, if you are informed, organized and diligent.

You will need to be resourceful in hunting out effective ways of promoting your book on a limited line of cash. It also pays to be creative in seeking out new avenues to your audience.

Having said all this, you may ask yourself, Why bother? Why should a person go through all that to publish a book of one's own? Let's consider that on two levels.

The Rewards

The first level is the internal, or personal, level. That is, in your own mind, what do you gain from self-publication? The matter of publishing a book, especially if you decide to undertake the project, is a tremendous learning experience. Furthermore, you don't stop learning; in fact, you don't *dare* stop learning. You will find out about things you would have never suspected otherwise. You become conscious of counterparts to publishing, and you will probably become more sympathetic to the situations of others.

But for a great many self-publishers, the primary reason for self-publication is control. If you sell your book to a publisher, matters are taken pretty much out of your hands. Someone else takes over the editing. It is harder for you to argue with someone else's editor, rather than the one you yourself hired to polish up your manuscript. Someone else designs the book; you have little or no voice in the design. Someone else decides the print run size. Somebody else makes the decisions regarding the promotion of the book. Somebody else decides how long the book will be promoted, and as a usual thing, larger publishers move on to other books after a year.

Then there is the adrenalin rush that comes when the truck delivers all those cartons (with so many books per carton) and unloads them in your garage. The buzz that comes from seeing articles and reviews about you and/or your book is quite intoxicating.

The satisfaction of actually producing an attractive book causes a warm, rosy glow, too. You get quite a thrill seeing your book on store shelves, and an even bigger thrill when people tell you, "I *loved* your book!"

How many authors never see their books in print? While it is true that 50,000 books may be published in a year, a relatively small portion of those were books that the authors themselves saw into being. It is an accomplishment of which you can justifiably be proud. To sell one thousand, five thousand, or—wonder of wonders!—100,000 is a heady experience. It is even more satisfying when the year's bank balance is in the black.

Equally pleasing is recognition. People look at you differently when they learn you not only have written a book but actually have published it. What a heart-warming experience that is! But remember, too, that one of the jobs of the author-publisher is that of expert, and because you are an author, you are an expert!

The other side is the external level—how does "the world" regard the book you have produced? You have done a good job. You carefully researched to see that there was a spot in the marketplace for your book. You wrote it with great care for accuracy and for enjoyable reading. You gave it careful attention and made wise decisions as you saw it through production. The gods were kind, and your book received much attention and good reviews. It was in all the places where it needed to be. You have met with some success, and the book is selling, maybe not the millions of copies of the mass market best-sellers, but still, it is doing respectably. The financial rewards are gratifying.

You can keep your book active on the backlist, where another publisher would have directed interest to later books. An active backlist title can prove to be quite productive over the years.

Your book is better publicized for the most part. The author is after all the best promoter of a book, and the larger publisher uses the author for promotional activities anyway. You are likely to continue promoting your book well past the first four to eight months of its public life, longer than a larger publisher's promotion.

Active and ongoing publicizing, particularly if sales are good, means more dollars for the author.

After making a second press run, the proceeds from my first book, *Roughing It Elegantly* bought a filing cabinet, a canoe and a computer in its second year. It also financed the production of its first sibling, *The Paddler's Planner*. If you have done your work well, it is not unreasonable to expect a 10 to 15 percent return on your investment.

The Risks of Self-Publication

Self-publication is not without risks. It is enormously time consuming. In the next chapter, we will look at the various roles a small publisher plays, at the many hats worn for the roles. In evaluating the situation for yourself, how many hats can you wear? We will look at the primary hats. Do you really have the time to devote to the promotion of your product? If you thought writing a book was time-consuming, keep in mind that was the easy part. Can you, or do you want to, wear all the various hats that are in the publisher's office? Do you have the means (that is, will the book do well enough) to pay someone else for the services that you are unable or unwilling to do? **Treasure your time—it is one of your major resources**, and try to be as efficient at doing these things as you can.

How fat is your wallet? Can you afford the money needed up-front to produce and launch your book? It would not be wise to strip your own financial assets for what is in actuality a risky business. The expectation of insufficient financial return is a perfectly good reason why publishers may be unwilling to publish your book. However, the independent publisher, if able to do most of the various tasks personally, can successfully publish a book that a larger publisher cannot. The smaller publisher is not paying all the overhead of salaries, workers' compensation, insurance and office space. Furthermore, the smaller publisher can shop, just as the larger publisher can, for cost-efficient work. Look for ways to double the bang for the buck or for the hour.

Another danger of the novice launching into publication is innocence, the unawareness of the numerous aspects and details that emerge. This unawareness can be corrected by diligent, assiduous, persistent study. Learn all you can about the trade so that you are as well equipped as is possible.

Overconfidence likewise can thoroughly do you in. You can tread too far into unknown territory too quickly and wind up thoroughly lost. Further, early sales may create a false sense of success. One of the worst possible things that can happen to a small publisher is to be faced with enormous popular demand. Financially, this sort of thing could break you quickly, and it has happened to others. If sales suggest great demand and you opt for subsequent runs, keep those runs within your own financial resources. Use a printer who can provide quick turnaround to help assure that you complete those sales.

Be delighted with early sales, especially if brisk. Don't bet the farm on repeating them. Books may be returned if the bookseller thinks they have sat too long on the shelf.

It's *your* project, your success or failure.

A Realistic Look at Income

Since you will be investing so much of your time, you may want to consider whether a publishing project will produce a reasonable return for your time. In short, don't give up your regular job to publish. You also need to have some idea of the financial returns you might reasonably hope to gain. Notice I said *hope to,* not *expect.* There are no guarantees that your project will make you any money. However, by your shrewdly determined strategy and careful preparations, you can greatly enhance your likelihood of making at least a small profit on the book.

Is The Price Right?

One of the first questions to ask yourself is, "Is the book priced right?" It is an important question. A book must be reasonably priced to the potential buyer. Your book should be within the general range of books of its sort—not too much more costly, and certainly not too much cheaper. Check out the prices of similar books in your local bookstores (they won't all carry the same titles). Setting the price for your book will be discussed in more detail in Chapter 6.

How About The Costs?

The other question about your book is, "Are my production costs low enough?" At this point, many novice publishers get themselves into deep trouble. Traditional lore in independent, small press publishing recommends that you keep production costs (cover design, typesetting, printing and binding) to between one-fifth and one-eighth of the list price of the book. For example, a book priced at $12.95 (the average price of a trade paperback in 1990) ideally should be produced for $1.62 (i.e., 12.95 divided by 8). Production costs certainly should be no greater than $2.60 (12.95 divided by 5). While the margin between sale price and production cost seems quite large, in reality it isn't at all.

In the first place, unless you have prepared for a humongous mail order business or if you are marketing to a highly specific target through special channels, most of your sales will be to the book trade (bookstores and libraries, which are actually two very different channels). You, as a very small publisher, will not be able to get at those sale points except through wholesalers and distributors. Without getting into the distinction between wholesalers and distributors (the lines are often quite blurry), suffice it to say that you essentially pay another company to take your books and get them into the hands that will get them to the buying public.

Wholesalers and distributors who sell to bookstores generally buy from publishers on consignment; that is, you don't get paid until they get paid—for the books *they* have sold. Distributors often have catalogs, costly to produce; sometimes they also have sales representatives. They have to sell to their buyers at a discount, and consequently they order from the publisher at a deeper discount. They handle the collection and fulfillment of orders. For their services, they may demand discounts of up to 60 percent of the *list* price of the book. On your $12.95 book, you may do well to get $5.18. Increasingly, the trend is for the publisher to pay shipping charges to fill those orders, and those costs run up quickly. Avoid the situation of some publishers whose production costs were so high that they could not afford to go through needed distributors.

A curious point on this is the matter of value perceived. If your primary market is in a particular type of specialty shop, you may very well be able to get more for it than if it were a general or a mass market title. Remember mass market titles are priced cheaper because the quantity produced leads to a much lower unit cost.

Watch that Cash Flow!

You need cash on hand during the early days of your book's public life, as the payments from those same wholesalers and distributors generally run anywhere from 90 to 120 days. (It is not uncommon for this period to run as long as 133 days.) In some instances, such as direct sales to libraries or individuals, or specialty outlets, you may be able to get payment in 30 days. On consigned books, generally the distributors send monthly reports of sales and then, two months later, a check for an earlier month's sale. That is, if your distributor sells five copies of your book in February, you will get paid for them in May.

Another unpleasant trait of the book business is returns. Unlike other items of merchandise, bookstore managers can, after three or four months, even up to a year, decide that those books have taken up space on their shelves long enough, and they will return them to their source. If payment has been issued for the books, a credit is expected, or in the case of one- and two-title publishers, cash.

Forecasting a Year's Sales

Since the beginning publisher has difficulty making a good estimate of or forecasting a year's sales, it is hard to develop a budget for the coming year. Without a track record, there is absolutely nothing to go on. Unless sales have been brisk and the cash flow abundant, it is difficult to project expenses for a new year. It isn't much better for the second year, either, as a great many variables come into play. One important variable is the number or placement of reviews that call attention to the book. Surprisingly enough, even though you may have done all the right things in getting review copies out to the proper spots, the desired reviews may not show up for months. This happened with *Dark Sky, Dark Land: Stories of the Hmong Boy Scouts of Troop 100* (Tessera Publishing, Inc.). Galleys for it went out in August, 1989; review copies went out simultaneously with the publication date of October, 1989. The highly influential *Booklist* reviewed it in September, *1990*, from the galley copy (more on galleys in Chapter 7), nearly a year after it was submitted. *Boy's*

Life Magazine reviewed it in February, 1991, a year and a half after publication.

What you can count on is that sales will sag during the third year. (Remember the life expectancy of a book?) What do you do then? Somewhere, sometime you must make decisions on the future of your publishing house. Do you increase efforts on promotion? Do you want to retreat from publishing or go on with it? Do you have another book ready for production? If you are left with more inventory than you think you can sell, do you find a dealer who will take the remaining books for a fraction of their price?

Can You Succeed as a Self-Publisher?

It is possible to succeed as an independent publisher. (You may determine your own definition of success.) Self-publication is not of itself vanity publication. John Muir started John Muir Publications of Santa Fe in 1969 to market *How to Keep Your Volkswagen Alive: A Manual of Step-by-Step Procedures for the Compleat Idiot*, hardly a topic for a self-centered person. Muir later moved over to specialize in offbeat travel books, with sales of $2.5 million in 1989. It is important to realize that independent publishing is an entrepreneurial venture. Not everybody is meant to be an entrepreneur, nor does everybody want to be. Are *you* cut out to be one?

An entrepreneurial venture first of all requires a good product—it is absolutely essential that you begin thinking of your book as a product even before you finish it. You must be able to detach emotionally from your book and view it objectively as something others would want to buy. Be rigorous in your examination of it, because having rigorously examined the book, having identified its strengths and worked to reduce or eliminate its weaknesses, you are able to project a strong belief in it. This is tremendously important. As stated earlier, you will be selling a product, and you must have faith in it to promote it fully.

You need to have strong organizational skills. Time is a valuable resource and should be hoarded. Can you undertake a project and sort out priorities on what needs to be done and when? Can you accomplish a task with a minimum of effort? We're talking here about the ability to organize and dispatch tasks ranging from chores with routine motions but little thinking, such as preparing a large batch of press kits—stuffing, addressing and stamping—expeditiously to the structuring of your working time.

How are you in the self-discipline department? Are you able to determine a schedule of activities and then see it through? The more you are able to be a firm boss with yourself, the better your chances as an entrepreneur/publisher.

Above all, you are going to need a certain amount of temerity, a willingness to venture (this gets to be a scary business to launch into). However, in the long run, the decision of whether or not to publish your own book remains in your hands. Only you can judge whether you believe you have the talents and characteristics, the drive to carry a project through, and the wherewithal to undertake and carry on the enterprise, and whether the end results are worth it to you.

3

The Many Hats of The Small Publisher

YOU spent a lot of time writing your book. If you decide to publish it yourself, you will spend what will seem like inordinate chunks of your time in your publishing activities. Like many people who have decided to publish their own books, you probably have come from some other career field. You should be aware that the decision to publish will launch you into a new and fairly demanding profession. As the entire staff of your new company, you will find that you will perform many jobs that you had never expected to perform. You will enjoy some of the tasks, but loathe others. The important thing is that each job is extremely important and should not be ignored. Following are descriptions of some of the major jobs you would fill if you were your own publishing house. The titles may be different in other publishing houses, but the tasks remain the same. Some functions are closely related so that in a one-person publishing house, the line may be nearly invisible.

Writer

Perhaps your book came about because you like to write, and indeed you consider yourself primarily a writer. You may have already tried to sell your manuscript to a publisher and have learned of the difficulties in getting a publisher's interest. People who consider themselves writers first and foremost often prefer to stay that way. As your publisher, you may want or expect you the writer to produce other books written. (If you have the time!) But you will find much of your writing time taken up by routine correspondence and the creation of promotional materials. A good cover letter alone can take at least a couple of hours to compose, and you will be writing many different cover letters, not to mention all the other writing pieces. Brochures, for instance, are time consuming to compose and design. If you really like to write letters, or enjoy creating copy, or can write a good press release, you can happily use your writing talents. There will be plenty to do.

Managing Editor

The managing editor of your publishing house oversees the preparation of the manuscript for final production. This includes copyediting, decisions about illustrations and other additional material. The managing editor should be able to recognize good material. Particular skills and talents should include strong background in language and grammar, knowledge of good language usage, a good sense of content organization, and the ability to determine whether the book's contents are conceptually coherent. Finally, the managing editor should be able to set and implement priorities.

In addition, this editor works very closely with the marketing manager in determining what projects will be undertaken.

Financial Manager

The financial manager's role is crucial; the wearer of this hat looks to see where the funds to finance this publishing operation are coming from, and monitors and manages the cash flow to insure smooth operation and to keep project spending within reasonable or desired bounds. The financial manager requests and evaluates bids on the book production.

The financial manager also doubles as the in-house accountant. This hat keeps the financial records, tracking whether your fledgling company is or will remain solvent. The role is particularly important since the financial manager is the financial decision maker. The financial manager also sets up accounts and deals with vendors.

If you don't like working with numbers and spreadsheets or are poor at keeping track of virtually everything, and if you lack self-discipline in money handling, you reduce your chances for a successful publishing venture.

Designer

For people with a strong visual sense, a strong sense of color and its psychological and emotional impact and a love of design, the job of designer can be great fun. For the book itself, you will be selecting the most appropriate typefaces, deciding where to put the illustrations that were chosen, determining the appearance of the pages, coming up with the ideas for the cover that will make a strong and effective presentation. These questions can, on the other hand, be terribly frightening and overwhelming to a person who has no interest or experience in that sort of thing.

Along with designing the book, you'll be designing eye-catching flyers and brochures.

If you feel you lack those basic talents, but that you can recognize and appreciate good design, have no fear: you can find a designer to steer you through these matters. (It *will* cost you money.)

Production Manager

The production manager sees the book through the production stages from the final manuscript to the finished book. This can be done through one of two approaches. The first is the Little Red Hen (very well then, I'll do it all myself) approach. Here, working with the financial manager, the production manager works out the economics of production, determines where to get the jobs done and awards the bids. What is it going to cost with a print run of 2,000? 5,000? How much can be spent on cover design? Who is the best printer, typesetter or prepress service bureau to work with? Who do local author/publishers use? Who are good local production people? Having chosen vendors for these tasks, the production manager works with them throughout production. Have you learned enough about production to know what questions to ask?

Then there is the "Let George do it" approach. "George" is a book packager or broker who shops for the typesetting, printing and binding work. If you live in a smaller city or town which does not have the extensive range of resources, finding George has much merit. Check the business phone directory of the larger cities near you. Or contact one of the regional publishers' associations (see Addresses) and ask for help in finding George.

You should, as production manager, develop and stick to a working schedule and work well with other people on a project.

If your answers for this hat are mostly "Yes," being the production manager need hold no terrors for you.

Marketing Manager/Promotion Director

The ability to develop a market is one of the most crucial aspects of successful publishing. The marketing manager watches the book market with an eye to trends, noting directions and sales levels. From that study, the marketing manager can determine whether the odds for a book are generally favorable.

Decisions about the manner of marketing are critical and should be a part of the identification of the book's audience. Do you have the necessary information to channel efforts toward effective marketing? Will the book be marketed traditionally, through bookstore channels? Or will it be marketed through less traditional book outlets? direct mail? The manner of reaching that audience will shape the nature of the marketing program.

In your small publishing house, the marketing manager also doubles as promotion director. Do you know how to reach appropriate people to promote a book and its author?

The marketing manager makes the world aware of this new book by promoting it through newspapers, magazines, radio and television. The job starts before the book goes into production and is ongoing throughout the book's life. Maybe you don't like the mundane business of seeing a book through production, but thoroughly enjoy getting hustling to make the world aware of your book and your author.

Sales Manager

The sales manager hopes the marketing manager has done good work, because good marketing and promotion pave the way for sales. It takes strong belief in the product and great energy and enthusiasm to be a good sales manager. The sales manager works with sales representatives, bookstore managers, distributors and people who sell through more non-traditional modes. The job requires being good at determining what people want and need and making that work for increased sales. If nobody knows about the book, the sales manager's job becomes *much* more difficult.

Distributor

The distributor sees that books go where the marketing manager and the sales manager have made openings for them. In addition, the distributor fulfills of orders that come directly to the publisher. In very small operations, the distributor also takes charge of all the financial records required with fulfillment. The distributor should be meticulous in keeping records of sales and shipments. With publication, the distributor may be able to pass the bulk of the work on to outside wholesalers and distributors.

"Expert"

This is one of the most pleasant jobs. Because they prepared thoroughly on the book's subject matter before publishing, experts are created when they write books. An "expert" makes the marketing manager's life easier by being comfortable speaking to the media and being readily available for public appearances. Recognition as an "expert" is not hard for the author to tolerate, either.

Secretary ("Grunt," "Go-fer," "Wife")

I think it was Gloria Steinem who said "Everyone needs a 'wife'," meaning everyone needs somebody to attend to all the mundane, boring details of life. This is the person who meticulously tends to all the tedious stuff—packing books for shipping, keeping up with all the paperwork that goes with a business and preparing invoices, shipping labels and billings. No matter what you call the person who sees to all the little grungy details—writing letters, dropping galleys off at the typesetters, going to pick up flyers at the printer, seeing to whatever arrangements have been made for promotion or distribution, filing, folding papers, stuffing envelopes, etc.,—this last position is at once the most important and the least satisfying. Speed and accuracy on a typewriter or computer keyboard helps. Efficiency in developing procedures for routine matters is valuable. The everyday details of a small press tend to be long on time consumption and short on job satisfaction.

4

Your Preparation and Training

IF you think the publishing project looks feasible, and if you do not have a background that gives you a head start in beginning a publishing venture, acquire one. The public library can be tremendously useful. I say "can be" because public libraries come in all sizes and smaller ones don't have the resources of larger ones. If your local library lacks material you need, talk with the librarian about interlibrary loans to get the books you'd like to use. Libraries belong to networks, and generally they can get books for you. You may have to pay for postage on these interlibrary loans, and it may take awhile for you to get the books you want. (See also Information Sources—Electronic Databases.)

You will need to know about editing, book design, production and marketing (oh, yes, you *must* know something about marketing). You may need to learn more about accounting and all the details of running a business.

Read!

The best books on self-publishing include those of Dan Poynter and Marilyn and Tom Ross. (See Recommended Reading—Publishing.) In fact, after reading this book, if you still are interested in self-publishing, get one of the above, or better yet, both. They cover essentially the same territory, yet each has emphases or elaborations on areas the other doesn't. Other useful books are listed in the Recommended Reading section.

For a broader understanding of the publishing industry itself, there are the materials produced by John Huenefeld. The *Huenefeld Guide to Book Publishing* is revised periodically, and anyone considering being a publisher should be aware of it. He also publishes biweekly *The Huenefeld Report*, which is for managers and planners in modest-sized book publishing houses (fewer than 75 employees).

If reading about the various aspects of publishing has not daunted you, read at least one of John Kremer's excellent marketing books, particularly his *1001 Ways to Market Your Books*. These books will give you a fairly precise and detailed view of the things that have to be done, and provide you a timetable for doing them.

You may also need to study specialized areas for successfully operating a business, such as accounting, marketing or promotion. Take some classes to equip yourself with the needed informational tools. Check out your area community colleges, vocational-technical schools or public schools' community education programs.

If you are serious about publishing, buy some of the books recommended; this is money well invested. You will find that you can't absorb all the information on first reading—much of it won't seem real or meaningful, especially if this is a new world for you. You'll want to be able to refer to these books from time to time as need arises (and it will!).

Keep track of all the books you buy and classes you take for business and tax purposes. Your accountant can advise you of various points you might not be aware of and their tax implications.

Trade Publications

Books on publishing provide core reading. It is useful to subscribe to some trade publications, too, if you are to succeed in the publishing world. The primary trade journal is *Publishers Weekly*. This magazine includes articles about trends and events in the book business. Further, *PW* reviews 75 to 100 books per week, or 5,000 per year, out of the 50,000 published annually. A small publisher prizes getting a book review in *PW*. Also, publishers use this magazine to announce books going out of print. *PW* is not cheap; current annual subscription rates are $119. Some of the larger libraries subscribe to it.

Another important periodical is the earlier-mentioned *Huenefeld Report*. This publication deals more with the workings of the publishing business from the inside. *PW* is concerned with the publication, marketing and selling of books, and is read avidly by the book trade. *HR*, on the other hand, follows the internal economics of publishing—reducing costs of production, profit/loss margins, salaries and wages, etc. As with *PW*, subscription rates are high, about $88 per year. As *HR* is a highly specialized periodical, you may not find it in the local library. If you decide to become a publisher with several books in your future, read *HR* with some frequency.

Writer's Digest might be useful for improving your writing. A primary goal of *WD* is to enable writers to sell their work successfully, a most laudable goal. However, its more useful parts for the publisher are those that deal with the market—areas of interest, hence potential niches to exploit for books.

Join Organizations

Trade Memberships

To become more involved in the publishing world, join a professional or trade organization. On a local or regional basis, you are able to tap into a splendid information network. Publisher groups vary in size and approach. Generally, an organization meets on a regular basis and publishes a newsletter. Other activities vary from group to group and with the particular board currently running the organization. Some associations hold monthly meetings with programs aimed at informing their members. Others on occasion hold special programs, seminars or book award programs. Some organizations engage in promotional activities such as producing catalogs of members' publications, special events such as large book signings, marketing programs and the like.

Several national organizations exist. The largest is the American Association of Publishers; its focus is on the larger publishing world. The novice publisher may prefer to delay joining it.

A more useful one is the National Association of Independent Publishers. It publishes a newsletter (*Publisher's Report*) and has an annual book competition. Annual dues are $100. Another is COSMEP. It uses an acronym of its earlier name, the Committee of Small Magazine Editors and Publishers, (which no longer accurately describes the group). The name change reflects a shift in the character of the organization, as it now bills itself as the International Association of Independent Publishers. COSMEP publishes a newsletter, acts as a clearinghouse for members organizing cooperative mailings. It also provides exhibition opportunity for its members at the annual American Booksellers Association (ABA) and American Library Association (ALA) trade shows. Dues for COSMEP are $80.

A relatively new organization is the Mid-America Publishers Association (MAPA), based in Lincoln, Nebraska. Since it is a regional group rather than a state or local one, it tends to hold occasional events rather than monthly meetings. One of their activities is an awards program designed for Midwest publishers to recognize excellence in several categories.

In the Upper Midwest, the Midwest Independent Publishers Association (MIPA) has a membership, not surprisingly, of primarily small, independent publishers. Counterpart organizations can be found across the country (see Addresses). You can find kindred spirits, many of whom have already published at least one book or are in the process of publishing; they are an invaluable resource of information, encouragement and comfort. MIPA's stated mission is to help its members produce high quality publications and be successful in their publishing activities.

Investigation will reveal other, more specialized publishing groups, such as religious, children's books, etc., if needed.

Marketing Memberships

Publishers Marketing Association (PMA) is a cooperative organization of publishers across the country that helps its members sell more of their books through a variety of marketing activities and exhibit services. As with COSMEP, the Association provides exhibit space at the two major trade shows. PMA's membership dues are scaled to the number of employees in a company. Dues for the novice publisher are currently $80, though combined membership in PMA and one of the state or area groups are offered at bargain rates.

Open Horizons, a company rather than an association, publishes the monthly *Book Marketing Update. Update* provides current information on editors and reviewers for magazines, newspapers, radio and television programs that have features about books. It also provides information on other sales avenues for the publisher. It is particularly valuable for people who do not have access to the large libraries that provide the annual directories (see Recommended Reading—Periodicals). Subscriptions are $48 per year.

Other marketing groups exist on a more or less regional basis.

Booksellers Associations

You may or may not wish to take out an associate membership in the American Booksellers Association (ABA); this is the trade organization for booksellers, primarily stores. The ABA holds the industry's major trade show. Each year at the end of May, book buyers from all over the world come to see what publishers have to offer. For the small publisher, it is not particularly cost-effective to join the ABA, or to rent exhibit space at the trade show, but you may want to tap into one of the appropriate publishers' groups mentioned above to exhibit your book at the ABA show.

An associate membership costs $125. Benefits include a discount on booth rental at the ABA's convention, registration at member rates for publishers that are not exhibitors at the convention, a magazine (*American Bookseller*), a weekly newsletter (*Newswire*) and rental of ABA mailing lists at member rates.

More to the point is membership in a regional association, perhaps more than one, if your book has sufficiently broad appeal. The Upper Midwest Booksellers Association (UMBA) serves Minnesota, North and South Dakota, Illinois, Iowa and portions of Missouri and Kansas. Membership dues are $40. Publishers and publishers' (sales) representatives make up a small portion of their membership. UMBA produces a newsletter and a holiday catalog for wide-spread mailing, and has its own show in September. Counterparts to UMBA are found in other sections of the country (see Addresses—Bookseller Organizations). Membership in UMBA or its counterparts provides an opportunity for a bit of visibility and for understanding bookstores' situations. As with publishers, there are specialized bookseller groups.

Ancillary Memberships

If you are not already a member, you may wish to consider joining and participating actively in a writers' group. Many writers find it helpful to join a group where they can get feedback and encouragement on their work. Group discussion of your work should help you sharpen its focus and clearly define your prospective market. It helps to have outside support (and not just financial), whether writing a book or publishing one.

Other useful memberships (and this applies to subscriptions to publications as well) include organizations that have some bearing on your book. Because Cat's-paw Press (the author's publishing house) publishes books related to canoe camping, the author has a membership in the Minnesota Canoe Association and subscribes to *Canoe* magazine and the *Boundary Waters Journal*.

Virtually every craft or activity has an association, and in addition to its newsletter, the association publishes a directory of its members. You can use this directory to announce the publication of your book to them. Often, you can rent their mailing lists. Usually, your local librarian will know if a directory pertinent to your area exists.

Learn Your Markets

Back when you were writing your book, did you think about the person(s) who would be reading it? If you haven't done so, by all means give it considerable and serious thought now. It is, however, very late in the game to think about audience at this point. This question should have been considered while, if not before, the book was written. As a bit of discipline, thinking of your audience causes you to sharpen your book's focus. Use "Friendly Readers"—people whose judgment and taste you can trust—for help in shaping your book. Generally, novice authors tend to be paranoid about someone stealing their ideas or stories, but there is no need to be too wary. Unless you have a most remarkable set of Friendly Readers, most people do not have the energy or the expertise to duplicate (or improve) your product. Again, a writer's group can be helpful.

Who Will Buy Your Book?

Where is this product going? Are you looking at the adult market? children? the sports enthusiast? Is yours the sort of book that has reasonable staying power or will it be out of date in two months? Is the book informational or is it a gift item? What is the age range on your target audience? Is it male or female or both? Is it a special interest book? Where will it be sold?

Judicious hunting can suggest whether there is a market for your book. Look at books on store shelves; check out the competition (i.e., check *Books in Print* for current titles in the target area); read appropriate magazines for reviews of comparable books. While you are at it, check out the prices and book sizes. Look for what unique advantage your book can have and *use* it.

When you publish a book, you can no longer think of it as a part of you. It is a new product, and you must discipline yourself rigorously to think of it as such. You must be objective.

Who Can reach that Buyer?

Once you know the people who would be likely to buy your book, think about where it should be so that they could buy it. When

I considered publishing *Roughing It Elegantly*, I made a list of places that could possibly sell it. Bookstores were an obvious choice, as were outdoor recreational stores. State and national park gift stores were naturals. Department store book departments were another possibility. I considered the book shelves some supermarkets maintain. One productive area I originally overlooked was library sales. Perhaps your book would be suitable for schools.

So again it's back to the library. (Yes, you *are* making many trips to the library; but you need far more information than you can get on a single trip.) Somewhere along this line, consider whether you are looking at single sales (as through direct marketing or single contacts) or multiple sales (as to retail outlets—bookstores, catalogs, mass market outlets such as grocery stores, or gift shops, libraries, etc.).

Determine the appropriate individuals at these places and find out how to get at them, and then how to get them to stock your book. This means learning how distribution systems work. The books on self-publishing by Dan Poynter and the Rosses go into some detail explaining distribution.

Make It Happen

To make these good things happen—selling all your books in a year or so—you must identify business contacts who will help you achieve your goal. At the risk of being repetitive, use the library. One of the greatest assets to a publisher is a large public library with a sizeable basic resource collection. Some of the resources that such a library will have include directories of booksellers, associations, publications, and the like. (See Information Resources for a listing of some of the directories available.) If you are not aware of what kinds of information are available—in print—educate yourself. Thinking of selling to gift stores? There are directories. Don't overlook the most familiar directory of all—the phone book. A major library will have an extensive collection of phone books, both white and yellow pages, of many major cities.

Naturally, it is not enough merely to identify these potential contacts (and don't forget that can be rather a time-consuming task). You now must reach them and tell them how great it would be for you and them if they would buy (or sell) your books. Call or write. (Is your stationery supply dwindling?)

5

Preparing the Manuscript for Publication

Whether you find a publisher for your book or decide to publish it yourself, the preparation phase will be much the same. It's time to get the manuscript into its final form prior to its metamorphosis to finished book.

What's in a Name?

Have you selected a title? Are you sure it hasn't been used already or is currently in use? Check *Books in Print* or *Cumulative Book Index* to be sure. (The 1990-91 edition of *BIP* includes over 130,000 new titles, and 115,000 titles that are out of print.) The title is your first opportunity to catch a would-be reader's interest; you don't want to waste the opportunity. Book marketing guru Nat Bodian cites cases where book sales bloomed and other cases where they died with a title change. Kathleen Meyer's book, *How to Shit In the Woods*, presents an interesting example. The cover and title as originally published were forthright, and, not unexpectedly, aroused a bit of an uproar. So Ten Speed Press, the publisher, brought out another cover that was less blunt, with the title *How to S— In the Woods.* At one point, the first version was outselling the latter four to one.

Final Manuscript Preparation

Once you have finished writing your book, you have completed the initial preparation phase. Your next major task is to see that it is in "clean" condition—typographical errors corrected, spelling, grammar and punctuation all emended. Even then, if you have not already done so, ask others, preferably those with a strong command of language structure and a strong critical eye, to read your manuscript. *You* know what you think you said; it is time for someone else to confirm that you said it in the clearest, most elegant manner. You need friendly readers who can help to strengthen the focus and sharpen the material. In many respects, they do preliminary editing. More to the point, they assist you in conceptual editing: Is the book coherent? Is the material properly organized? Have you resisted the temptation to throw in all the material you discovered, whether it adds to the thesis of the book, simply because you went to an awful lot of work to get it?

The process of editing a manuscript is more extensive than many people realize. The obvious part of editing is to catch mistakes in grammar, spelling and punctuation. Good, knowledgeable editors also catch errors of fact or point out inconsistencies in information or points of view, and become valuable allies in the composition of your book. They point out weak spots in presentation, suggesting terser explanations, more elaboration, or a need for the apt anecdote or illustration.

You should choose an editor who has some understanding of your book's field, particularly if the field is technical. Finding an editor can take anywhere from twenty minutes to weeks, depending on your resources. In larger cities, you may find a chapter of the Professional Editors Network, or a comparable organization (ask your librarians). Failing that, go to your local newspaper (pick the largest), and ask the managing editor if there are editors on staff who free-lance. If you have a college in your area, contact the English department. Talk to the composition instructors rather than the literary instructors because composition teachers are attuned to the sorts of things that your manuscript needs.

While you can reduce many small goofs in your manuscript with a spelling checking program or one of the newer grammar checkers, it is a mistake to rely on them completely. Spelling checkers highlight words they don't recognize, but they don't recognize flat-out wrong words. For instance, they do not differentiate between "our" and "out." Recently, I read about a water-skier pulled along while holding onto a "taught" rope! Rely on your trusty dictionary. Spelling checkers may or may not catch repeated words (e.g., the the).

You can expect editing costs to run from $30 an hour up, depending on what you want done with your manuscript. You can expect the job to take at least ten hours. When you interview a prospective editor, the two of you should thoroughly discuss what needs to be done, so that you both come to a full understanding of your book's focus, what the editor is to do, what the compensation rates will be and some notion of how much time it may take. It is proper and advisable to ask to see work that the editor has done or to ask for references. Agree on some sort of schedule, especially if you will be producing the book fairly soon. Don't forget to acknowledge your editor's work in your book.

What is the format your manuscript is in? Is it typewritten, or better still, do you have it on computer diskette, with a printout (hard copy)? Using a computer to store your manuscript is most valuable since it is so much easier to correct, add or delete material, and to generate copies as wanted. The advantages of diskette storage extend to the typesetting phase, discussed in Chapter 7. Even if a publisher produces your book, you will find the editor has a strong preference, for the economy of it, for receiving the manuscript on a compatible diskette (with a printout, too).

Beyond the Manuscript

The text of the manuscript itself, however, is not the whole story or the only consideration for your book. Some details are basic, such as the front matter. The nature of the book's content also will bring up some additional matters to be addressed.

Gathering The Front Matter

The front matter comprises all the pages up to the beginning of the text proper. It includes the half-title page, the verso (or back) of the half-title page, the title page; on the verso of the title page is the copyright page; next is the dedication, if any. The Table of Contents includes appended material such as bibliography, notes, or index.

Essentially, the copyright page contains a biography of the book (see illustration, Typical Copyright Page). Vital parts of this biography are the book's copyright date, author's name, Library of Congress number, Cataloging in Publication data (which includes subject categories), ISBN, and printing history. Where applicable, the copyright page lists illustrations (and illustrator), and additional credits, such as editor, printer or book designer.

Copyright ©1986, 1989 John Kremer
All rights reserved.

Published by:
Ad-Lib Publications
51 N. Fifth Street
P. O. Box 1102
Fairfield, Iowa 52556-1102

Printed and bound in the United States of America

Library of Congress Cataloging in Publication Data

Kremer, John, 1949-.
1001 Ways to market your books: for authors and publishers.

Bibliography: p.
Includes index.
1. Books—Marketing 2. Publishers and publishing
3. Authorship 4. Self-publishing

I. Title II. Title: One thousand and one ways to market your books.
III. Title: One thousand and one ways to market your books.

Z278.K72 070.5 88-083673

International Standard Book Number 0-92411-20-1
International Standard Book Number 0-92411-19-8 (pbk.)

Typical Copyright Page

Library of Congress Number

Back to the letter writing. Write to the Library of Congress (see Addresses—Book Numbers) to request preassignment of a Library of Congress catalog card number. Request the form for obtaining the number and in time, they reply to your request with an assigned number. This number belongs to the *work,* no matter its form—hard cover, paperback or Braille edition. The first two digits indicate the year of assignment. There is at present no fee for this. You will receive the appropriate form and a kit describing the cataloging in publication (CIP) procedures.

At the same time, write for copyright information. This comes from the U.S. Copyright Office, also a part of the Library of Congress. Register the copyright after the book is published; the fee for copyright registration is currently $20.

Cataloging-in-Publication Data

The CIP data block is a little more complicated. If your book is nonfiction, it is crucial to have it properly cataloged for libraries. Librarians, as well as booksellers, like to know how to categorize books in order to shelve them properly. The CIP data block enables them to do this. In the past, the Library of Congress has performed the task of determining the cataloging-in-publication data. Currently, the Library is swamped with cataloging requests, due in part to tight budgets (Congress hasn't increased its allocation for several years) and in part due to the burgeoning numbers of publishers. The Library has long been averse to cataloging the work of self-publishers, and the budget constraints have not helped.

This is not an insurmountable obstacle, though. Look at books in the local library to see how the CIP data block is organized. List the author's name and the complete title of the book. Then, add information such as whether there is an index, a bibliography, illustrations, etc. Use other books as patterns. The publisher *should* be able to state in a couple of words what the book is about. These words are cataloging information called "subject tracings" and help locate a position on shelves for a book. Again, look to see what words and numbers other books similar to yours have. Note the numbers listed in similar books. Two are cataloging numbers (the first is the Library of Congress classification number; the second is the Dewey Decimal number); the third is the Library of Congress card number. Finally, the ISBN is listed.

Look at the page sample (Typical Copyright Page) showing the Library of Congress CIP block. Provide the author's name, year of birth (and death, if applicable), and the ISBN data. The tricky part comes in the line just above the ISBN. The first number is the Library of Congress catalog number. Note that it contains a letter, followed by a number, a decimal point, another letter and a final number. The letters and numbers are coded to categories (though the second letter is the initial of the author's last name). The second is its Dewey Decimal number, which is widely used by librarians to shelve books, and the final is the Library of Congress number. Talk with a librarian about applying numbers to your book. If your book is on camping and the library has several on the subject, the general category numbers should apply. Determine what seems to be appropriate and cross-check with a librarian. For about $35, you can get a librarian to look at your book, ask a few questions that you should be able to answer about the book, and assign it the appropriate numbers.

The ISBN

Write to R. R. Bowker (see Addresses—Book Numbers) to obtain an International Standard Book Number (ISBN). R. R. Bowker is the agency that monitors and assigns ISBNs in this country. Essentially, an ISBN is to a book what your social security number is to you. Every book, every form (paper or cloth) of a book, every edition has its own ISBN that serves as its identifier for ordering and stocking purposes to booksellers and librarians all over the world. It is essential that you get one for your book. An ISBN consists of ten digits. The "shape" of the ISBN indicates how big a block of numbers has been assigned to a particular publisher, and the larger the publisher number, the smaller the publisher. To illustrate, Cat's-paw Press is a small press. The ISBN for this book has the number 0-9618227-2-4. The *0* indicates that Cat's-paw Press is an English language publisher. The next seven-digit group (9618227) is Cat's-paw's publisher number. Larger publishers have smaller publisher numbers. A very large publisher's books' ISBN might look something like this: 0-934-55555-5. The next to last number is the title and edition number, and the final number (which is linked to the title number by Bowker in the assigned block) is a check number. The title and edition numbers are assigned by the publisher from the numbers assigned by Bowker.

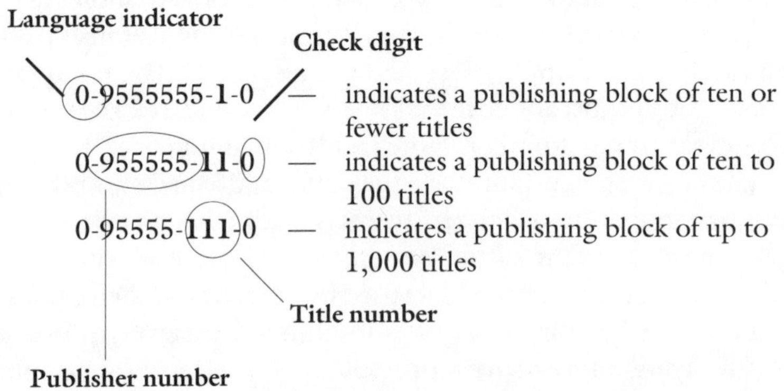

The "Shape" of the ISBN block

A new publisher should write a letter on his or her letterhead requesting ISBN assignment. In *The Self-Publishing Manual,* Dan Poynter recommends asking for 100 numbers (the assignments are in blocks of 10, 100, 1,000, etc.) because if you do get serious about publishing, you can use up ten quickly. The information sheet returned will ask for publisher name, address, and other pertinent information about the book in question. In addition, Bowker follows up periodically requesting Advance Book Information (the ABI form), which is used to keep *Books in Print* up to date. Bookstores use the microfiche of *BIP* to locate books requested by customers that they don't stock. Bowker also produces an even more massive listing of titles on a tiny form with their *Books in Print* on CD-ROM.

Earlier, there was no charge for the assignment of publisher number and ISBNs, but times and costs have changed, and now there is a $100 fee to a new publisher for a block of numbers. They are not the swiftest people to respond to queries, so write early for your numbers.

Dates for Books

Dates are important for books. Two particularly important ones are a book's copyright date and its publication date. What should the strategy be?

A work is essentially copyrighted once it takes a tangible form, when words started going down on paper, but the copyright *date*, which appears on the copyright page, will be the year of publication. It is not uncommon for a book with an autumn or early winter publication date to appear in time for the holiday market, yet have a copyright date for the following year. The situation is something like that of automobile models; the 1993 models appear in autumn or late summer 1992.

However, for the book reviewer, the publication date is tremendously important. The publication date does not appear in the book, but it is listed in the ABI forms and is mentioned in all the publicity materials. For this reason, publicity materials going out for your new book should always state the publication date (month and year) for the book. Reviewers don't like to review old stuff. (There's another good reason for setting the publication date several months later than the expected production of the book. The later date gives reviewers reading galleys ample time to do their work, and you can then use any glowing comments in your publicity materials.)

The Library of Congress number is also a dating device. The first two numbers of 87-070138 indicate the year a book went into production (here, 1987). It is understood and expected to be the same year as the publication date and listed copyright date.

Illustrations

Are illustrations an important part of your book? Will they be line drawings? Maps? Photographs? Graphs? Cartoons? Don't short-change your book by failing to support the text with appropriate visual materials. The manuscript to *Dark Sky, Dark Land: Stories of the Hmong Boy Scouts of Troop 100* (Tessera Publishing, Inc.) is a vivid set of oral histories of young boys escaping from their war-torn homeland of Laos. A map of the region was essential to give the reader a sense of the book's setting.

Do you know exactly where in the book you will place these visual materials? Who is producing them? What permissions are required and have you acquired them to use the materials? Have you acknowledged the sources in your book? The sources may object to your use without their being acknowledged or compensated, and they may demand recompense. This can be a pretty sticky area, so it would be wise to investigate legal ramifications that may crop up.

References? Bibliography? Index? Other Materials?

Does your book have or should it have references or a bibliography? Does it cry for an index? If you think your book should be a part of a library's collection, give it better chances for such a destination by providing those items.

If references or bibliography are appropriate, you no doubt have been collecting those items all along with the writing of the book. Consult a style book, such as the *Chicago Manual of Style* (see Recommended Reading—Editing), for the way you should organize that material.

The matter of an index, though, is something else. An index is a valuable tool in a book, since its purpose is to enable a reader to find information quickly. The tricky part is *how* that index is organized. Will a person who approaches the index think about the desired information in the same way as the indexer (or the author)? Consider whether to rely on the indexing capabilities of a good piece of software (some of the good word processing programs can index), whether to use the services of a professional indexer, or a combination of both. Book marketing expert John Kremer recommends that the author do the indexing, arguing that the author knows best what is in the text. The *Chicago Manual of Style* has a highly pertinent section on indexing, what it should do, who should do it, and how to go about it as a do-it-yourself project.

It could also be argued that the author is too close to the material to do a proper job. (An excellent case in point is the index to most any computer software manual.) There is a national association of professional indexers, and most states have at least one chapter. Check at the library for a directory of indexers available in your area. (See also Information Resources—Organizations.)

Traditionally, an indexer works from the printed keylined text, and therefore index creation is a last-minute task. Expect to allow from two to four weeks for this job, and then allow time for the result to be typeset and printed. The cost of indexing depends on how technical the work is and the book's length. A charge of $2.50 a page (finished book-size page) is not uncommon. For *Roughing It Elegantly*, the indexing cost was about $160 (in 1987).

6

Starting Your Business

To produce and sell books, you must set up a business. You probably already have a work space that you will transform into the home office (literally as well as figuratively) of this new business you are creating, and we will talk about its needs. But first, let's create a business.

Naming Your Company

First, you must decide what to call your new venture. Selecting the name by which your company will be known requires careful consideration. While John Wiley and Alfred Knopf did very well with companies bearing their name, independent publishers are advised not to use their names as company names. It fairly shrieks of self-publication, which tends to be a drawback. Since the name will project a certain image about your company and even about the type of book or books you will publish, it is fair game to use a bit of imagination. For instance, there is Permanent Press. I liked the name Garlic Press Marjorie Knoblauch chose for her cookbook company. The whimsy in choosing the name of a common kitchen tool appealed to me. The real cleverness emerged later when I learned that "Knoblauch" is the German word for "garlic." The name of Dan Poynter's Para Press came from his first book, which was about parachuting.

Consider whether the name will be easily understood on the phone. It should be clear and reasonably sensible. Incidentally, it is fun to watch the same sort of free wheeling attitude in the naming of television production companies, which share a certain number of problems and attitudes that small presses do.

While at a bookstore or the library, survey publishing company names for ideas. When you have arrived at some sort of decision, check *Books in Print—Publishers* to see whether or not the name is already taken. Cat's-paw Press, publisher of how-to books, has on occasion been confused with Cat's Paw, Inc., publisher of computer books, and vice versa. Likewise, check with your state's department that deals with business registration and register your proposed name. This is called filing an Assumed Name (the name assumed or taken on for a business) or something similar that conveys the idea. Currently in Minnesota, my home state, the fee for this is $25, plus about $25 for publishing the Notice of Assumed Name in a local paper (the charge is about $4.50 per column inch). Simply call the appropriate office and fill out the application sent to you. In Minnesota, the appropriate office is the Secretary of State. Other states may organize differently. If you don't live in your state's capital city, check your local library for that city's phone book to get the address and phone number.

If you have the finances to hire a designer to create a company logo, that's wonderful. A logo projects an image of you and your company, and a well-designed one is a tremendous asset. It is, however, an item that can wait. Hiring someone to design a logo can run anywhere from $150 to $1,500.

Determine the Company's Structure

You have several options for the structure of your new company. You may choose to organize it as a sole proprietorship, a limited partnership or a corporation. Investigate the specific characteristics, and the advantages and disadvantages of the various types before you become a publisher. States vary somewhat in their definitions of and requirements for each type. This is definitely a matter for discussion with your accountant. Whichever type you choose, you must register your business with the state.

Basically, a sole proprietorship allows you (as the sole proprietor) to put money into the company and take it out as you wish. You are responsible for reporting profits or sales taxes to the federal and state tax offices.

A limited partnership likewise has rules governing it. A limited partnership is a partnership in which the limited partners share in the partnership's liability only up to the amount of their investment. As the term "limited" implies, there are several specific bounds. If only you publish your book, this type of business is irrelevant. If you take on a partner, work out the necessary agreements with good legal advice, as the nature of a partnership is complex.

A corporation becomes an entity unto itself. It may or may not be worthwhile for an individual to organize the business as a corporation since recent tax laws have made incorporation less attractive. Too, there are variations to the corporation, depending on the nature of the business involved. However, if several people, particularly unrelated people, are involved, a corporation is generally the best way to go. By all means, consult with an attorney about setting one up. Before the business is established, the participants should have a *written* list of specifically who is to do what, and be in agreement with those ideas, compensation, and the eventual dissolution or termination of the corporation (to name a few items). Corporations are registered by filing Articles of Incorporation.

Minnesota has a Small Business office which publishes a helpful free book aimed at helping individuals start up a business. Many other states have similar organizations. You will need to apply for a state tax identification number.

Also, if you hire an employee, either full or part time, you will need to get federal and state employee identification numbers. Guidelines will accompany the ID numbers, too.

Another source of advice is from the Service Corps of Retired Executives (SCORE). Local chapters of this organization offer seminars and workshops designed for small businesses. (See Information Resources—Organizations.) It may also be possible to get individual and personal help to set up your company. Check with the chapter near you.

Finances

Money may be the root of all evil, but it is also what makes it possible for a business to grow. Where you get the funds to publish your book, how you apply them and the general cash flow are all crucial to the publication and distribution of your book.

Where Does the Money Come From?

Any business enterprise needs funds to get going. Possible financial sources include personal savings, financial help from friends and relatives, grants from foundations, and banks. The sale of books will generate some income, but at this point sales are not a reliable source of funding. Banks as a rule are not friendly to lending money for book publishing. Unless your manuscript fits in well with the general scheme of a foundation, your chances of getting help there are extremely slim. The competition for grant money is horrendous, and special skills are needed to write grant proposals.

Do you want to borrow money from friends or relatives? If so, make it a business loan, and set up a schedule for repayment. Are your own savings sufficient to launch this enterprise without leaving you financially strapped and vulnerable? Remember we are talking a *minimum* of $10,000, most of which will be drawn on in a space of about three months.

Develop a Business Plan

Earlier I asked, What are your goals? If one goal is to make money, you need a plan for your business. The plan can be highly simplistic—decide what the appropriate market outlets are for your book and determine how to get at them. However, a better idea is to develop a more comprehensive plan. After all, you do get to where you want to go quicker if you have a precise set of directions. Books are available that will give you the appropriate frameworks for a business plan. *A Guide to Starting a Business in Minnesota* (from the Minnesota Small Business Assistance Office) has a sample business plan. (See Recommended Reading—Business Planning.) Or read Starting and Managing A Small Business of Your Own from the U.S. Government Printing Office. (See Recommended Reading—Business Planning, where other books are listed as well.)

Along with your business plan, formulate a company mission statement. A mission statement, first of all, states the *reason* for your publishing house's existence, and making this statement should give you real pause for thought. As you brood about your purpose, be sure to wear your marketing manager hat while considering. Trailblazer Books has a clear mission statement: "helping children and adults explore, appreciate, and understand Minnesota's natural heritage." Trailblazer publishes Minnesota map books and an adventure travel game. Its primary author, Dr. Constance Sansome, also has a published book on Minnesota geology that is a classic in its field. The field laid out in the mission statement is closely focused, yet wide enough for a small but steady stream of titles for eventual publication. If it were the choice of the company to expand, the mission statement could be widened to encompass a region rather to this essential task, depending in large part on your personal temperament.

The first approach is to decide how much money you have—a specific sum—to put into this project of publishing and promoting your book. Having determined this, allocate specified portions to the various phases of the project. The percentages listed in the table below give rough but useful approximations. I should note that personally, I include preproduction expenses (editing, design and the like) as part of the basic cost of producing the book. The figures are demonstration figures; some categories may reach higher numbers. I should also point out that these are *production* costs: none of these figures include any sort of compensation to the author.

The percentage is obtained by dividing the item expenditure by the total expenditure. (A computer spreadsheet is useful here. Set up the categories as listed in one column; enter the projected expenditures under Amount. Under Percentage, enter the formula for dividing the item by the total. The cost per unit (CPU) is based on a print run of 3,000 copies, and is obtained by dividing the total expenditure by 3,000.

	$ Amount	**Percentage**
Pre-production expenditures		
Book design and cover	$2,000	11%
Typesetting	$ 800	8 %
Printing and binding	$4,200	40%
Additional pre-production (e.g., indexing)	$ 250	2 %
Post-production expenditures		
Promotion	$2,000	19%
Fulfillment	$ 985	9 %
Overhead	$1,000	10%
Total	**$ 10,435**	

Cost per unit $ 3.48

Publishing Costs

You can expect that virtually everything will wind up costing more than you had anticipated, so it is well to build in a "fudge-factor" as a cushion. In the example above, the overhead costs (operating costs, office expenses, equipment, phone, postage, etc.) is a good place to build in this cushion. Some publishers add 10 percent to each item in the projected expenditures calculations to accommodate for unforeseen cost overruns.

The second approach to setting up a budget is to determine how much money you need to do the things that must be done, and then go about securing the funding. Either way, you see where the money is going.

At a fairly early point, estimate what it will take for you to break even—recover your costs—on this publishing project. Note I said "break even," and nothing about profits, nor about paying for your time.

Start with the *retail price* of your book. This is, at this point, a hypothetical number, approximating what similar books sell for. Calculate that the *average selling price* will be about 45 percent of that. The other 55 percent accounts for variables such as the cost of distribution and marketing. So if you determine that $11.95 is a reasonable retail price for your book, calculate that its average selling price (ASP) will be $5.38.

From that $5.38, you subtract the fixed costs of producing the book. Fixed costs include art work (book design, cover, illustrations, maps), editing, indexing, typesetting, printing a specified number of copies, publicity, and incidentals. (Points of view on what to include in the fixed costs vary; the table above goes at it a bit differently.) Add up the fixed costs and divide by the number of books to be printed to determine the fixed cost per unit or copy (FCPU).

Divide the fixed cost per unit by the average selling price (ASP) to find your break-even point. Again taking the example of an $11.95 book, assume, for the moment, that the FCPU is $2.33, or about $7,000 for the print run. The break-even point is 0.43, or 43 percent of the run. That is, on a print run of 3,000 copies, you will break even when you sell about 1,300 copies. If the book described in the example lists at $11.95 and has an ASP of $5.38 , it will take sales of nearly 2,000 copies for you to break even. If the book were priced at $14.95 with an ASP of $6.73, the break-even point would come somewhere between 1,500 and 1,600 copies sold.

Setting the Price of Your Book

You see from all this that the price of the book affects these calculations. Set the price of your book by going shopping. Go wherever books are sold, particularly those of the same sort as yours, and look at their prices.

Pricing is tricky. Too low a price will not persuade people that it is worth buying. If your book, for instance, is aimed at a business market, a low price may cause it to lose credibility. If, on the other hand, it is a short-lived book, too high a price will deter potential buyers.

Most importantly, the book must be properly priced so that you can come out without losing money on each sale. The price of the book is the base line for calculating your production costs, which will be discussed in Chapter 7. The traditional rule of thumb for small press is to keep your production costs to one-eighth of your *list* price, or no more than one-fifth of list. In the table above, the FCPU is $3.48. The retail price would range from $27.95 to $17.50, expensive for a garden-variety paperback. Look at your projected expenses to see where costs could be effectively cut and still allow you to produce a good book *and* have enough money to promote it. (Ample promotion is a *very* important consideration.)

With the price of $11.95 that we used in the above example, the FCPU of $2.33 is one-fifth list, which narrows your working margin and hence potential profitability. The importance of careful shopping and planning to cut those production costs is plain. Don't get yourself caught in the same bind others have found themselves in. They found their production costs were too high in relation to list cost, so that they literally could not afford to get their books into the normal distribution channels.

Organize Your Office

Along with naming your company and determining finances, you will need to set up your office, too. The space need not be fancy—more than one independent publisher has an office in a spare bedroom. The basic needs are a place to work and a place to put things, preferably fairly close at hand. You need desk space, book shelves and a filing cabinet. If you already have a computer and printer, they have their own space (more about computers and printers later). A large, walk-in closet is a great place to store packing materials, promotional materials, and ideally, several boxes of your books for convenience in filling small orders.

Stationery is of the earliest things you will need to purchase. Once you begin requesting bids for materials, references or any of the thousand and one things that crop up, you'll need your own stationery. You should have letterhead stationery, envelopes and business cards, all with your company name, address and a phone number. Don't worry at this point about a fax number. If you find that you send material by fax often, find a nearby outlet and put that number on your phone file for ready reference. Purchase a nice quality paper—not necessarily the most expensive—for your stationery, as that too projects a message about your company. Lots of 250-500 are a reasonable start. While you get a price break on larger quantities, you may not need them. You will need more envelopes than letterheads.

Some fairly typical costs on basic items follow; keep in mind that shopping may produce better prices. Stationery paper will run about $60 per 500 sheets (or $80 per thousand). Don't forget to get plain paper (for second and third sheets) to match. Matching #10 envelopes (a useful size) will run about $66 per 500 envelopes. You'll use five hundred in a relatively short time. Having a logo applied to any of these items will generally add about a $30 setup charge per item to the initial printing cost. On subsequent printings (by the same printer), though, the cost reverts to the basic printing charge. You should also purchase business cards with your company name, address, phone number and your name, which will range between $20 and $35 per 500, depending on how fancy you want them.

You'll also need office supplies with your letterhead printed on them. You can keep the cost down on these if you use simple printed material that includes the information you have on your cards. You will need packing slips (invoices). I prefer the two-part, carbonless ones, which run about $66 per 500. For billing invoices or statements, I get the four-part carbonless ones (8⅞-x-7 inches in size) for about $90. Quantities of 500 should be adequate for your first year. These need envelopes (#10 with windows); cost is about $38 per 500.

You need mailing labels for the packages and boxes of books you will be shipping. They cost about $27 per 1,000, again with a $30 setup charge for the first order.

You will need mailing and shipping supplies. It takes awhile to get a sense of the sorts of quantities you will be shipping. At first, it may be cheaper to buy boxes and envelopes in small quantities (one to five items). It is certainly fair game to scrounge and recycle boxes acquired elsewhere. When you begin buying boxes or packing envelopes in quantity, you will find that boxes each cost $0.62 and up, depending on the size of the box and the quantity purchased. (A side consideration is where will you store those supplies when you graduate to the larger quantities.) Tape for closing the boxes is about $1.75 a roll, less if you purchase larger numbers of rolls. Some vendors throw in a tape dispenser with the purchase of a certain quantity. Find out the packaging requirements of handlers. Remember that both the Postal Service and companies such as United Parcel Service use automated equipment in handling packages, and string just won't do.

Packing envelopes, such as the large (9-x-12-inch) plain Tyvek® will cost about $0.50 each (in quantities, $20 per 100). Padded envelopes will cost from $0.22 each up, depending on size and quantity (quantity may be based on 250).

And of course, we haven't said anything about the basic, everyday office supply needs. If you haven't already got one, get a rotary file, such as a Rolodex™ ($12 up). You will need file folders ($5 per 100), and copy or typewriter paper ($5 ream). You probably already have such things as paper clips (assorted sizes), desk scissors, calendar, etc. Don't forget to keep track of purchases of these homely little items as business expenses.

Keep current records on everything. You are:
(a) running a business and
(b) promoting a book.

Tracking Systems

When you set up your business, you will also set up tracking systems (see Computer Records for publishers). You will need to follow inventory (this is, after all, a tangible asset). Naturally, you will be tracking all sales—when, to whom, on what terms, date and amount paid, and sales records for state sales tax reports. You will develop mailing lists and some system of maintaining them. If you do not already have a computer, you might want to give serious thought to getting one. Computer experts advise first selecting software (programs) that will do the jobs that you want done, then the computer that will run that software. However that may be, people who are interested in desktop publishing find that the Macintosh (which has been widely regarded as overpriced) offers ease in use and an abundance of programs to do what needs to be done. Others prefer the IBM or IBM clones when used with appropriate software. Don't get a computer just because you are thinking about publishing a book. That isn't a good reason for making such a major investment.

Software programs vary widely in cost and capability. My feeling is that the cheapest is not usually the best choice. You can quickly outgrow programs with limited features. A versatile program with many features can lure you into finding your own uses for them.

You can manage very nicely with three pieces of software. The first is a good word-processing program for correspondence, further manuscript writing, publicity materials and the like. One popular and powerful program is Microsoft Word, available for the Macintosh and IBM/IBM compatible machines, and generally easy to use. There are others, such as MacWrite II and WordPerfect. Prices for word-processing programs fluctuate. Their power has increased over several updates. Currently, you can get Word or WordPerfect for about $300, street price (in catalogs or at discount houses). The list prices are substantially higher. (You may detect a bias toward Macintosh computers; these are familiar to the author, and eminently workable for the novice publisher. There is also an abundance of good programs for publishing with a Macintosh.)

Second, you will need a spreadsheet program for setting up your financial records. Some good accounting packages are available, but if you are new to all this, a spreadsheet is a tool that you can use to record transactions, track inventory, make projections and do basic calculations to determine a project's feasibility.

The third major item is a database for recording your developing mailing lists. (See Computer Records for Publishers for a more detailed explanation of what sorts of records to keep.)

An old war-horse of a starter package for the Macintosh is Microsoft Works, an integrated package that contains a word-processing module, a spreadsheet and a database. (Integrated means that you can switch from one module to another and transfer data without having to close down one module and open another. Integration is useful and convenient.) Later integrated packages, including Works, include more sophisticated capabilities.

Microsoft Works's spreadsheet is a somewhat abbreviated version of Excel, which sold separately retails at about $300 (catalog price). (Works also has telecommunication capabilities, which I have not found necessary yet. At some point, I will no doubt get a modem or a fax, maybe both, but I have not yet seen a need.) Works has the beauty of being relatively inexpensive (retailing at about $200).

Other integrated packages receiving high marks in computer magazine reviews are BeagleWorks, GreatWorks and ClarisWorks.

Quicken is another well-regarded business accounting program, available for both Macintosh and IBM/IBM compatible machines. Its most immediate asset is its capability of keeping close track on where the money come in from and where it goes. How effectively it does this depends on the precision of category defining you do. It also can be used to track inventory, though considerable effort goes into linking the inventory ledger with sales accounts. One other major asset is that Quicken is inexpensive (under $50).

As you become more and more adept in using your computer and its programs, you may want to move up to more sophisticated programs. Keep in mind that you can expect to spend a couple of hundred dollars a year in updating programs and equipment. You will also find it useful to acquire special utility programs to use with your other applications.

An abundance of public domain software offers possibilities at low or no cost. Read the appropriate computer magazines or find a computer user and see what is available. A word of caution: Get a program that destroys the various types of "viruses" that may be introduced into programs, and apply it before using any public domain or otherwise acquired software. A virus can do some nasty things to your programs or records.

Having a printer as well as a computer is highly dependent upon your financial resources. Fortunately, printer prices, like computer prices, have dropped considerably over the past few years while their capabilities have increased. You will need to print out many documents, from manuscript drafts, to letters, business forms to mailing lists. (True, you could use a typewriter, but a computer saves much repetitive action. You can manage with a good quality impact printer (dot-matrix or daisy wheel) for everyday tasks, particularly where you will be making multiple copies of things such as invoices, but as soon as you are able, purchase a second printer. Start with about $500 for a dot-matrix printer, or about $1,000 for a laser printer, and go up from there. Study your needs and goals, shop carefully and don't rush to buy. In our office, we use an impact printer for printing multiple-copy forms, and a laser printer for correspondence.

Storage Space Available?

To store large quantities of your books, you need a dry, safe storage space. A well-enclosed garage can be better than a basement (it is also easier to have the books delivered into the garage than lugged downstairs). How much space will you need? As an example, the printer delivered 2,000 copies of the 200-page paperback *Remembering The Women of the Vietnam War* (Tessera Publishing, Inc.) in cartons containing 64 copies each. A carton measured 13 x 19-x-8 1/2 inches, and there were 32 cartons (one wasn't full). Preferably, the cartons should rest on the wooden pallets they were shipped on to keep them off the floor. You can store 3,000 books (similar in size to the one described above) in a 4-by-6 foot space without having to stack too high.

Storing your inventory close at hand has its advantages; orders can be filled immediately. There is something, too, about having a space that is identified as the business office of your publishing company! However, be warned. As your company's activity increases, you find that you never have *quite* enough room. Ah well.

7

Your Book Appears!

Now that you have your manuscript polished up, your marketing education proceeding apace and your business created, you are ready to launch into the exciting and scary phase of getting the book into production for presentation to the wide, wide world. You will discover that things can get pretty involved now, but they are manageable if you can keep a firm grip and maintain a sense of calm.

All phases of production first involve collecting bids from vendors for each aspect. Shop carefully. Get *at least* three bids on any project.

Develop a request for quotation (RFQ) outlining what you want done on each phase of the project. With this basic request form, vendors can reply (bid) and you can compare their bids. It is entirely possible that after receiving a few responses to your RFQs, you will find that what you thought you wanted won't work. Revise your want list and send out new requests.

Getting Physical—Production

Now that your book is about to acquire a physical reality, you will have considerable control over its size and look. Book design has several facets, and we will take them in turn, starting with the outside. This is also where the *big* expenses emerge.

How Big Will it Be?

Unless there is an extraordinarily good reason to choose otherwise, select one of the six basic book body sizes. These standard sizes (in inches) are 5½-x-8½, 6-x-9, 7¾- x-10½, 7-x-10, 8½-x-11 and 9-x-12. The first two sizes are commonly used for trade paperback books. (The size that fits those racks in supermarkets is smaller than any of these.) Sizes other than these will create some difficulties in the printing stage, and the cost of printing will go up considerably.

Your book's third dimension is how thick it will be (this has bearing on the cover design, as it determines the width of the spine). Count *every* page—text, photos, illustrations, blank pages, front matter, *everything*!—and try to have the total in multiples of 16. This is called a *signature*. Sixteen (or sometimes 8 or 32) is a magic number. To see why this is so, take a sheet of paper, fold it in half once, then fold it again. You will see that if you cut the first fold, you would have four sheets, or eight pages. So it goes with additional folds. The size of paper the printing press uses determines whether it processes signatures of 16 or 32 pages.

A book of 128 pages contains 8 signatures, an efficient size. A book of 120 pages will use most of 8 signatures, leaving a few pages blank. Such pages can be used to quote remarks about your book, include an order blank or provide a place for the reader's notes. A book of 135 pages presents a problem: it could be printed in 8½ signatures, with a couple of blank pages. Half-signatures are not a serious problem, but they will incur some extra expense. It would be best to make adjustments before you go to press. Discuss how your vendor prefers to deal with split signatures.

Note that the number of *book* pages is not the same number as the number of the *text* pages.

The Cover

At an earlier point, you determined your likely readers. You also should have determined how to reach those readers/book buyers. The cover design you select should enhance your chances of getting them to buy your book. Design your book toward your intended market. Check out the book offerings in nontraditional booksellers, such as recreational stores, if that is the direction of your book, or whatever area your book might be sold in. Spend some time (maybe even a little money) looking at books on topics that interest you in bookstores. Books meant for the book trade (bookstores) often look quite different from books sold primarily by direct mail. (This is no small consideration; over half the books sold in this country are sold by direct mail. *Time-Life* and *Reader's Digest* Books, to cite only two, have extensive direct mail campaigns. See Recommended Reading—Marketing.)

You have several fundamental decisions to make, and for the

self-publisher, cost is a major factor. Use color on your cover, as a black-and-white cover can be boring. The decision to use one color, two colors or four colors will rest partly with the nature of the cover design. The use of two colors (for instance, black and green on white paper) is not as stark as it seems. Remember both colors can appear in a range of color intensities. More is not necessarily better than less; four-color will cost more. (You may have to read up on color printing a bit to appreciate what is involved here.)

Are you going to use pictorial material on your cover? Pictorial material includes drawings, paintings, photographs or maps. It isn't essential that you include such materials—examine covers of books that you find attractive, and absorb the parts of the design that work. You'll find many appealing books that use only graphic renditions of type.

Your cover indeed, all your illustrative elements—should be appropriate to the tone and content of the book. When *Roughing It Elegantly* was "under construction," I thought hard about what would be on the cover. Because so many books about Minnesota, and particularly about Minnesota's North Country, had covers with photographs of a woods-surrounded lake, generally with a red canoe on it, I knew I wanted something that would be different, yet would be faithful to the content of the book. So I settled on a painting, which eventually included a lake shore, a (yellow) canoe, and a traditional Duluth pack in the foreground. Since I am no artist, I went to a cover designer. The cost was fairly substantial, about $1,100, but it proved a good investment. Numerous booksellers have remarked on the handsomeness of the cover. Expect to spend anywhere between $500 and $1,500 for cover design. The industry average, according to Heunefeld, is about $700 (1990). I suspect the low figure is due to larger publishing houses having in-house designers and are thus able to produce cover designs more cost-efficiently.

Also, either you, or someone you pay, will write copy for the back of the book. This is actually your book's built-in billboard, and you should exploit it. Many people will pick up a book, automatically turn it over, read what is on the back, and decide whether or not to buy.

Patrick Redmond, this book's cover designer, says when he designs a cover, he keeps in mind how it would look in a black-and-white, postage-stamp sized version. If you decided to advertise your book, your budget may not allow for a large ad, yet you want your book to appear in it. A person should be able to read the title even when the cover design is reduced.

Also, when you hire someone to design your cover, choose a person who is well-versed in the peculiarities of book covers. The designer should ask you questions about the perceived audience and should be aware of the implications the design will have on the book's marketing.

How do you find a designer? Check metropolitan libraries for the *Encyclopedia of Associations* to see if there is a graphic design association near you. Also, identify publishers in your geographical area and ask them for names of designers. You can also check with schools for commercial artists for names.

If you are completely new to this field, hire a highly skilled and experienced designer; you can learn much from such a person.

Bar Codes

A bar code has nothing to do with one's behavior in a pub. It is now an essential part of a book cover's design. The bar code is a symbol placed on the back of the book, capable of being read by an optical scanner, to provide a specific set of information about the item bearing the code. Bookstores, particularly the big chains, increasingly demand bar codes stating price and ISBN on books. Basically, there are currently three types of bar codes that may be used on books. Mass markets such as discount and grocery stores use the UPC, or Universal Product Code, as they are not so much interested in tracking the sales of a particular title, but rather are interested in the vendor (i.e., the publisher). This is not particularly useful to the small publisher. Then there is the Item Specific UPC code, which identifies the vendor (publisher, with the ISBN publisher number) and the book title as well as the price. However, in the book trade, the standard bar code is the EAN Bookland code. The EAN Bookland bar code identifies the publisher, title, and edition (through the ISBN) and the price of the book.

Larger cities have one or more businesses that provide bar codes for the diverse requirements of business. Check your phone book for companies under "Bar Coding." Newsletters for publishers' organizations also carry ads for companies providing bar code film masters. Again, a trade association contact can clue you in to vendors. Currently, the cost is about $20 for an EAN Bookland bar code. This is the one you will use if you expect to sell your books primarily through bookstores. For the Item Specific UPC code, a central source needs more information in order to supply a vendor number, etc., and the cost for acquiring that is more than $100.

Other publications such as audio tapes, videos or calendars are treated much like books. They too need ISBNs (or ISSNs in the case of periodicals), publication dates, bar codes and copyrights.

Book Design

The look of the book's inside is no less important than the outside, and the starting place is the selection of the typefaces. Ever remember starting a book that you "just couldn't get into reading"? With a rather surprising number of books, particularly early editions of the classics, the problem was not really the subject matter, but the typeface and size used. Choosing a typeface is one of the most arcane and bewildering areas that you can get into. Most everybody recognizes type in boldface and italic, but often that's about as far as it goes. A little clarification of terms might be helpful. A *face* or typeface refers to the *style* of the letter or the character of the type, in short, what it looks like. A *font* refers to a given typeface in a particular size. Computer companies confuse the issue when they say their computer has 19 fonts. What they may actually be providing is four *typefaces* (e.g., Helvetica, Courier, Symbol and Times) in a couple of different sizes and perhaps bold or italic.

The advent of the computer and word-processing demanded faces that could be easily read on-screen. For those unfamiliar with how such things work, here's a simple analogy. Imagine a piece of screen wire, one inch high and three-quarters of an inch wide. This corresponds to the space for creating a single letter. Then imagine taking a paint brush and carefully filling all the holes between the wires of the screen so that you produce the letter or character you have in mind. The finer the screen, the more holes that must be filled (the more dots, or pixels, there are), and the character will have a nice clean, sharp edge. But if the piece of screen has only nine holes in the vertical direction and six in the horizontal, you can immediately see that the look of the letter is directly affected. The earlier printers for computers were dot-matrix printers, simply because this reproduced essentially what you saw on the screen. Dots per square inch (dpi) is still what people are talking about when they speak of resolution. The starting points for printers now is 300 dpi, with high resolution being 1,200 dpi or more. Without getting technical about it, refinements in coding for producing letters and laser printers have greatly improved the resolution even in 300 dpi printers.

The point of this digression is that with printers capable of higher resolution than had been available some years ago, strong interest in attractive typefaces grew. Designing typefaces is something of an art form. Over the centuries of moveable type, many faces have been designed, and some have become classics for their beauty and readability. These classic faces in turn have become starting points for computer use design.

Finding out about typefaces may involve several field trips to printers or prepress service bureaus. A printer will show you samples of a given paragraph printed in the house's assortment of typefaces and sizes. Study them carefully, not so much for the intrinsic differences among them, but for what you find pleasant to your eye and easy to read. Read about typefaces if this is an unfamiliar area for you. Several useful books on type are listed in Recommended Reading—Production.

Keep in mind that some typefaces are designed for easy reading on the computer screen and are not necessarily meant for printing. Boston and New York (fonts with city names are generally intended as screen fonts) are examples and are included here simply to illustrate the differences in type appearance. Further, type is produced by several companies, and their versions of a basic typeface family may vary. The point here is that careful selection of typeface is important. Any of the noncity name faces are eminently suitable for book text, and they are not the only possibilities.

Let's illustrate with some of the typefaces available to a computer user. (With the burgeoning of the desktop publishing capabilities, a truly astonishing range of typefaces is now available, though the average computer user may not want to spend the money for what may have only limited use.) The size is 11 point type (the text of this book is 11 point Galliard). (The quotation is from *Roughing It Elegantly: A Practical Guide to Canoe Camping*.)

(Courier)

It had been a day of hard work; fallen trees had blocked the trail on several of the portages. That can make life difficult if the tree is large and you are carrying a canoe or a good-sized pack. At any rate, that was all behind us for today, and we had reached Trail Lake, our destination.

(New York)

It had been a day of hard work; fallen trees had blocked the trail on several of the portages. That can make life difficult if the tree is large and you are carrying a canoe or a good-sized pack. At any rate, that was all behind us for today, and we had reached Trail Lake, our destination.

(New Century Schoolbook)

It had been a day of hard work; fallen trees had blocked the trail on several of the portages. That can make life difficult if the tree is large and you are carrying a canoe or a good-sized pack. At any rate, that was all behind us for today, and we had reached Trail Lake, our destination.

(Palatino)

It had been a day of hard work; fallen trees had blocked the trail on several of the portages. That can make life difficult if the tree is large and you are carrying a canoe or a good-sized pack. At any rate, that was all behind us for today, and we had reached Trail Lake, our destination.

(Bookman)

It had been a day of hard work; fallen trees had blocked the trail on several of the portages. That can make life difficult if the tree is large and you are carrying a canoe or a good-sized pack. At any rate, that was all behind us for today, and we had reached Trail Lake, our destination.

(Times)

It had been a day of hard work; fallen trees had blocked the trail on several of the portages. That can make life difficult if the tree is large and you are carrying a canoe or a good-sized pack. At any rate, that was all behind us for today, and we had reached Trail Lake, our destination.

You should also think about page design in your book. Where will the page numbers appear? Do you want the chapter titles in headers at the top of the page? Do chapter headers go on the right- or left-hand page? Will placing subchapter heads at the top of the page make the book's material more accessible to the reader? Take the time to examine a number of books, particularly those that have some relation to your book. Use those produced by larger publishers as examples. See what the *Chicago Manual of Style* says about those details. Find the best looking and most authoritative books to use as your models.

Next consider the layout of your book. This has to do with the organization and placement of everything in the book. Naturally, with chapters, you will arrange them in the appropriate order. Do you want every chapter to start on the right-hand page? Where do the illustrations go? Do you want some sort of graphic element to mark chapter beginnings? Your ultimate objective in book design is to make your material easily accessible and pleasing to the reader.

Typesetting

A publisher has more options today than even five years ago. Then, to publish a book for the commercial market, a publisher had no choice but to go to a commercial typesetter. If the typesetter had high standards, with careful proofreading by both the typesetter and the publisher, a good-looking product could be expected. Eagle-eyed proofreading was essential, as errors could be introduced at the original stage of setting the type, or in the correction of errors, and lines or even sections of the type could be misplaced.

I wrote my first book on an Epson QX-10 in its VALDOCS program. This presented a couple of problems. The typesetter I was working with had printing equipment using IBM MS-DOS, incompatible with my machine. I had to get "translations" of my disks into

ASCII code that the IBM could read. Then the typesetter went through the whole manuscript putting in all the necessary formatting commands that laid out paragraphs and pages. (Which is still what typesetters do from diskette.) For those services, the fee was $1,200 for the 176-page book, or about $6.82 per page.

If you do not have a computer, you still can make use of some of the technology. If your manuscript is cleanly typed, take it to a prepress service bureau where it can be run through an optical scanner. The scanner reads your text electronically and translates it into a computer-compatible format and transcribes it to diskette. A printout gives you a "hard copy" so you can see what needs to be corrected. These corrections can be made on the diskette file, and the diskette and hard copy handed over to a typesetter or prepress service bureau for formatting.

Recently, I had a piece of printed material scanned. (It was a list of about 600 addresses.) The price quoted was $0.60 per thousand characters, or approximately $50. To give you some notion of what that means, this chapter contains approximately 49,000 characters. The price for scanning it would be approximately $30.

If you consider buying a word-processing program, you would be well advised to choose one that is fairly widely used. You increase your problems (and your expense) when a prepress service bureau or typesetter tries to transport your files into their preferred programs. Programs mentioned in Chapter 6 are widely used.

As an aside, I strongly recommend that you read about type and typesetting on a personal computer so that your manuscript and eventual book look professional. Learn about how to make "smart" or printer quotation marks and apostrophes, em dashes, and the like. It will help keep your book from looking amateurish and self-produced. Robin Williams has written two excellent books on this very matter: *The Mac Is Not A Typewriter* for the Macintosh user, and *The PC Is Not A Typewriter* for IBM machine users. Both are listed in Recommended Reading—Production and the one appropriate to your situation is well worth the price.

The Macintosh computer introduced major changes in book production. Other computer and software companies picked up on the innovations, and revolutionized the whole industry. With those developments, electronic, or desktop publishing (a term many users dislike), was born. Len Fulton (of Dustbooks, which produces directories of small publishing companies) noted that desktop technology allows small houses to produce books that look as good as those of the major publishers. An author may write his or her book on a computer and save the manuscript to diskette. Then several options are available.

Some publishers like to control the look of the book. One option is to acquire a page-layout program such as Aldus PageMaker or QuarkXPress, learn to use it, and then import the manuscript text into the program. One can be as creative as one likes. With these programs, you the author/publisher can produce copy that, when printed out, is camera-ready for the printing process. (Bear in mind that the quality of the camera-ready copy directly depends on the quality of the printer.) With their page layout capabilities, you skip the keylining phase of the traditional process. (Keylining too is expensive; bids for *Roughing It Elegantly* ran to several dollars a page or several more dollars per hour, depending on how the bidder approached the job—*and that was in addition to the cost of typesetting.*)

This software option has the double disadvantages of cost and time-consumption. PageMaker is not a cheap program, with list prices in the neighborhood of $700. Some catalogs offer it for around $500; QuarkXPress is even more expensive. QuarkXPress is often preferred by people who work a great deal with graphics. (IBM/IBM-clone owners like Ventura Publisher, which retails currently for about $800. Harvard Graphics is another powerful program, selling for some $400, discount price.) Program prices constantly shift as makers upgrade their products. I have found it worthwhile to upgrade the programs I own because the features added are useful.

Furthermore, these programs are not at all simple to learn. Powerful programs can do many nifty things, but you will spend hours discovering just how to use them, and deciding *what* you want them to do. While learning a new software program can be fascinating, it is also exasperating and time consuming. This book was produced on PageMaker, and I would hate to tell you how many hours I spent setting up pages in producing it. An advantage to owning a publishing program is having it available for producing smaller pieces. PageMaker and Quark are highly sophisticated programs. With patience in learning their capabilities, you can produce handsome brochures or flyers.

If your book does not require much beyond straight text, you can do quite a bit with more modest programs that are in the $150-

$300 category (list price: street price will be less). These programs are well suited for producing brochures, flyers and newsletters. Some of these (for the Macintosh) are Ready, Set, Go! (from Letraset), RagTime Classic (Ragtime USA, Inc.), Personal Press (Silicon Beach Software), and Publish It! Easy (Timeworks, Inc.)

Don't overlook the capabilities from the formidable word processing programs such as Microsoft's WORKS, WORD, MacWrite II (from Claris Corp.). They certainly can do *much* more than simple correspondence. Each program upgrade offers more useful features closer to many of the basic features of the page layout programs such as PageMaker, QuarkXPress and Ventura. For the IBM/IBM clones and prices in the $150-$350 range, there are the highly regarded WordPerfect (about $260), Professional Write ($165, SPC Software Publications), Microsoft's WORD (about $200, or $315 for the Windows version).

If you choose to hire a commercial typesetter to set your book, make a list of typesetters and draw up an RFQ. The basic question to ask is, How much will it cost to get your book from manuscript to copy camera-ready for the printer?

Nothing is ready, even with everything on diskette, until a hard copy, or printout, is produced. The printer is a major factor here. Generally, a person approaching the idea of publishing would not want to buy a high-resolution (1,200 dots per inch) laser printer; that is an enormous investment, though a lower-resolution (300 dpi) printer is useful for the daily chores of letter writing, press kit materials production, and the like.

With your manuscript on a computer diskette in a Macintosh or an IBM-compatible format, again you have options. One is to take your diskette to a commercial typesetter. More and more have acquired systems that link personal computer output to more traditional, high-quality typesetting machines. The costs on work prepared in this manner range all over the place. In shopping for *The Paddler's Planner*, which I had developed on my Macintosh, I received bids that ranged all the way from $800 to $2,800!

The production manager of a well-known, mid-sized publisher said that their usual practice is to have the final manuscript on diskette, a general layout (or dummy) of what the book is supposed to look like, a specification (or style) sheet that contains instructions for the type font and size for text, captions, headings, etc., and placement of captions and illustrations for the typesetter, who translates all that into the desired form. The typesetter produces camera-ready copy, with laser proof, for about $5 per page. (The page that the production manager was describing was for a 40-line per page, 6-x-9-inch book.) The cost of producing the camera-ready copy of a 176-page book would be about $880. (Contrast that with my original typesetting costs—$1,200—for *Roughing It Elegantly.*) Costs will vary, and it pays to shop.

An interesting development is the emergence of prepress service bureaus. Store-front printing shops frequently have computers available for short-time rental (in house), with the capability of printing computer data through a high-quality printer. This means in many instances a high-resolution (1,200 dpi or finer) laser printer, which produces clean printouts of your book that go directly to the printer for production. The service bureau people may take the diskette of your manuscript (all polished up and ready for typesetting), import it into their program of choice, format the book, and print out your camera-ready copy for the printer. For this sort of work, they charge about $60 per hour. Essentially, they have become typesetters of sorts. Negotiations at the outset are in order.

If the service bureau has a high-resolution laser printer, and you have your book completely formatted in a desktop publishing program compatible with their systems, you can get camera-ready copy at a reasonable price. Check with the vendor about the type fonts used in their system and compatibility with those used in your manuscript. If both are not alike, what you get may not be what you provided. Remember I spoke of different type designers? Several companies may design from a classic face and use the face name, but other technical matters lurk unseen, and one company's Times face, for instance, may not look like another's. The difference may not matter, but you should know why it happens.

Talk to the vendor before you decide.

Here's another recent development. Several printing houses make it possible to take the diskette files of the manuscript in final page-layout format and do the print job from that, essentially bypassing the intermediate stop of formal typesetting or the prepress service bureau. There is some time saving here.

If you are doing a simple personal project such as a limited edition of your family history, you don't need one of the first-line desktop publishing programs. You can keep costs down, yet produce a nice-looking publication with adept use of page layout capabilities of WORD or any of the better word-processing programs.

Printing

Printing is the largest single expense in publishing a book. Traditionally, the printers able to do the job at the lowest cost are in Michigan, close to major paper producers. Increasingly in the Minnesota area, printers are becoming more competitive. Submit requests for bids or quotations (RFQ) on the cost of doing the job to *at least* three printers before settling on one. (Books on self-publishing provide sample RFQs.)

In your RFQ, describe what you want done and what you have for the printer. You will state the book size (dimensions), the number of pages, type of binding desired, cover stock (the kind of paper for the cover), color work necessary for cover and/or book, illustrations that need separate attention (photographs, color illustrations, etc.), and weight and grade of paper (here you get into arcane matters of opacity and bulk). Ask them how long it will take to do the job, and to estimate freight costs for shipping the finished books to you. The printer will want to know the *form* —camera-ready, or film, or whatever—of the layout. There may be other considerations, depending on the nature of the book. It is important to talk with the printer before you decide. Don't be surprised if the responses to your RFQs come back in rather different form from the way you asked questions. Each printer has a somewhat different way of calculating work.

Be flexible on several points. Papers vary enormously, even what you think might be ordinary plain white paper. Some work better for books than others. Shades of white differ. Consider the bulk characteristics. Consider opacity. Does the text on the back of the page show through? Paper weights differ, a factor some publishers consider seriously, as it affects mailing or shipping costs. Paper has grain, and insisting on a book size that is not what the printer is well set for can result in paper being cut off-grain, with unattractive results.

Increasingly, books are printed on acid-free paper, a feature librarians love. Acid-free paper means a longer physical existence for a book. Printers are also responding to a demand for increased use of recycled papers, though there is considerable looseness as yet as to what constitutes paper that is called recycled. Discuss papers with your printer and pay attention to any advice given.

Inevitably, there will be mistakes (some of them yours) and extra charges. Last-minute changes or decisions on your part can run costs up in a hurry, not to mention producing unwelcome delays. Control what you can.

One vital point in choosing a printer is experience. Does this printer often manufacture books? Not all printers do, by any means. As in most other fields, printers specialize. If the printer doesn't offer to show you samples of books they've done, ask to see samples. It is certainly fair game to talk to *their* customers. There is no point in all of you being beginners on this project.

Starting a book through its print run sets it into a timetable or schedule. Commonly it will take anywhere from three to six weeks, depending on the printer's schedule and equipment. It is important that you understand what is involved at these points and that you deal with your part in a timely and prompt manner. This is a thoroughly real instance of time being money.

Print Run

How large should that first print run be? Print too few and it's soon back to press; further, the price break of a larger run is lost. (It is interesting to watch for stories where the initial print run of a book was a modest couple of thousand copies. The book catches on, and subsequent print runs will be two or three times as large.) Print too many and you may be paying for many extra copies. A story about Thoreau has it that he told a friend that he had a library of a thousand books; they were, however, all the same title (his). Despite heavy promotion and sales in the tens of thousands, the publishers of David Stockman's book on his experiences as Ronald Reagan's office of budget manager overestimated the market for the book, and wound up with a *surplus* of 200,000 copies! An industry survey (1987) of 31 publishers of assorted sizes reported that, on average, the first print run of a new book was 12,027 copies. The range of print run was from 3,000 to 30,000. (They considered any book with sales from 10,000 to 50,000 a best-seller. The median for the designation of best seller was 37,708 copies.)

A major consideration is what you can afford. On surveying the bids received for *Roughing It Elegantly,* it became clear that the unit cost dropped sharply between 1,000 and 3,000 copies. (I settled on a run of 3,000 copies, with a price of $3,840 for printing and binding. That was in 1987; the cost has gone up considerably.) While the cost dropped further at a run of 5,000, the total tab was more than I cared to invest at that time, especially since I had no idea of how well the book would sell.

A second consideration is anticipated sales. If you have no real notion of how well yours will go, much less whether, you might be much more comfortable with a print run of 1,000 or 1,500. If the book sells quickly, go back to press at a smaller per unit cost, as on subsequent print runs, the cost is printing alone. You have already paid for the cover and the typesetting.

It is not a good idea to print more than you can reasonably expect to sell in a year. (You don't want your money tied up and inaccessible. The savings on per unit cost of 10,000 copies is lost if 8,000 sit in your office for three years, since your money is tied up.) One mid-sized publishing house in the Midwest aims for a six-month inventory of a title! Bear in mind that they have a much clearer idea of how rapidly their titles move.

When collecting bids for a print run, whether a first printing of a brand-new book or a reprint, identify not only what the book sizes are that the printing house presses print best and find out the preferred press runs. For instance, one printer may be keenly competitive on a 5½-x -8½-inch size, but may not be geared for a 6-x-9-inch size. Another may not be set for short runs (under 2,500). If you are thinking of producing hardcover as well as softcover versions, be sure to let the printer know your intent. Consider binding only part of the books intended for hard-covers. If the hardcover edition sells well, then you are able to respond appropriately when you need more. Or if you need more with paper covers, you have the books. (In any event, have the printer run an extra 200 covers for promotional use.) Even if you decide to arrange for the binding yourself, discuss this with your printer, as that makes a difference in the way print runs are handled.

Binding

Another major decision is whether to produce your book as a trade paperback or as a cloth-bound (case-bound, hardcover) book. Producing a cloth-bound book is substantially more expensive. A paper jacket may be expected, though not necessarily required, with its attendant design, paper choice and printing, running the cost up higher. Hardcover binding generally adds about $1 per unit to your production costs. Choosing to produce a hardcover book means also making choices about several variations of binding.

Unless your book is meant for permanent collections, you should chose to produce a good-quality trade paperback. The old argument that libraries don't like to buy paperback books no longer holds. Many large libraries rebind paperbacks if they think the book needs it, and generally it is cheaper for them to rebind a paperback than to buy the hardcover edition.

If you have decided on a paperback edition, you have several options for the binding. A common choice, and very serviceable, is the perfect binding, which is simply binding the cover to the spines of the signatures (printed sections of the book) with glue. Books need to be at least a half-inch in thickness for this process to be used. At the present time, this is the least expensive way to bind a paperback book.

For some books, being able to lay it open flat is an important factor. One (and in my view, ugly) solution is the plastic comb (PVC) binding. It is suitable and appropriate for very short runs (under 150 copies). A spiral binding is somewhat more expensive than perfect binding. The Wire-O or double wire binding also is more expensive (it added $0.19 per copy to the production price of *The Paddler's Planner*, a significant portion of its $1.38 cost), but looks nicer and is more durable than the spiral binding. Bookstores and libraries are not fond of any of these mechanical bindings, with the primary objection being the absence of a printed spine. One way around that is the use of a wire binding with a wraparound cover. The wrap extends around the side of the book opposite the wire spine and tucks in under the front cover. Thus you have both a spine that can be printed with the title and still have the capability of a book opening perfectly flat. Other options are appearing.

One of the most exciting is Otabind, which was developed in Finland in the 1970s and introduced in North America in 1988. In the perfect binding process, the traditional method for paperback books, the cover is applied directly to the backbone of the book block with adhesive. The usual adhesive was hotmelt glue, which dries quickly and allows book blocks to be trimmed immediately after the cover is attached. Another type of adhesive, the polyvinyl acetates, provide greater durability and flexibility than hotmelt and, going on cold, don't require as much care in application. But being water-based, they take longer to dry.

The Otabind process combines features of both older methods. A book bound in this process lies flat when opened, yet has a spine that can be printed on. This answers the need formerly met by the wire and plastic bindings and dissolves the objection to them by librarians and bookstore people, who want to see the title on the cover's spine. Better still, the solid spine doesn't flex and crack like a perfect-bound book.

While Otabind costs more than perfect binding (up to $0.10 per book), it is cheaper than the mechanical bindings like plastic comb, spiral or double wire.

Manufacturers find that Otabind is used most efficiently in runs of over 4,000. For smaller press runs, Rep-Kover (a process related to Otabind) was developed. Rep-Kover (reinforced paperback cover) is available, but is somewhat more expensive than Otabind. As more publishers choose either of these processes, the cost may continue to come down.

Make Your Schedule; Set Your Calendar

Managing time is as important as managing money. Understand the importance of making a schedule. Set your schedule, or calendar; determine when you want certain things to have happened. (Is the cover design work done? Is the typesetting done? When should the galleys be out? What is your promotion timetable?)

Items on your schedule must mesh with the schedules of those you are working with. If you fail to have your material ready at the time determined earlier by you and the vendor (typesetter, printer, binder, whoever), you throw everyone's schedule off. If the vendor is delayed in getting at your material, your schedule is disrupted, and this can cause increased costs.

Build in ample time for proofreading into your production schedule, and allow time for indexing, if an index is planned.

Time is of the essence and the essence is money.

Launching and Promotion

At the same time that the book is going into production, you should be doing a great deal of groundwork to present it properly to the waiting (would that it were!) world. In preparation for this phase, you will have prepared your lists of the publications (this becomes a database) that should receive either an announcement of the new book, a galley copy (this is sent out *before* the book goes to press), or a review copy.

Several databases are useful. (More on databases in Computer Records for the Publisher.) One of the first that you should develop is a list of where to send prepublication galleys or copies. You can collect this information from the books on self-publishing. For your promotional program, develop another list of publications that should receive press releases and/or letters accompanying review copies. This list takes a great deal more work to develop, as you will identify the publications that are appropriate and the proper people to contact. Tailor your lists to your books. What's more, this is never a finished list. You'll find there is always somebody else or some other publication that you hadn't known about that should be there (see Information Resources).

You will have been collecting for some time your own lists of places to send announcements of your book's publication—friends, associates, relatives, local or area newspapers, local media spots—wherever you think you might get some interest. Likewise, compile a list of local and area book reviewers, feature writers, radio talk show hosts, etc., (addresses *and* phone numbers) who might write about or mention your book. Don't overlook appropriate magazines, either. More and more magazines have a column on books relating to their particular interest, and editors have to fill those columns. In fact, maintaining these lists should be a continuing process. Just as never being too rich or too slim, you can never have too many possible opportunities for promoting your book.

With the announcements, the simplest thing to do is write a good, exciting press release announcing the book's publication and reproduce the desired number of copies. Individually addressed envelopes (not labels) look nice if you have the computer and printer capabilities. This will rapidly deplete your supply of letterhead envelopes. Postage expenses will escalate, but they are a cost of promotion and a legitimate business expense. If you have extensive sets of contacts that you intend to send announcements to, find someone to help with the chore of addressing, stuffing, licking and envelope-stamping. I've done much of that sort of thing while watching a television program.

One objective of sending out galleys and preliminary copies is to acquire positive comments and testimonials about your book that you can use in promotional materials. Actually, you can and should use anything that comes in then or later, but it is nice to receive comments or testimonials beforehand, so the best quotes can be printed in your book.

All this means an enormous amount of writing, and good writing takes *time*. You must write cover letters for galleys and review copies focused toward the particular needs of the intended recipient. Assemble a press kit that contains the following items: a copy of the press release or announcement of the book's publication and a page or two of background information about the book and its contents. The press kit also should include biographical material about the author since there are hopes of the author appearing on radio or television or being interviewed for a print piece. Write or call radio and television personalities to interest them to invite you as a guest to talk about your book on their shows. Since most of them have limited time to read your book, it is fair game to include in the press kit a set of proposed questions that you would answer or talk about. Ideally, there should be black-and-white glossy pictures of the author and the book. (These don't need to be large: a 5-x-8-inch or 3-x-5-inch photo works just fine.) It looks more impressive and professional if these items are in an 8-x-12-inch folder. There is no need to be terribly fancy with the folder.

Find a company that reproduces photos in quantities to get copies made of your good "author" picture and of your book cover. To prepare the press kit folders for my first book, I spent about $150 for photos and folders, which has assured me of a more-than-ample supply of both.

As soon as you can get at it, prepare a brochure or flyer about your book. A flyer is a good way to introduce your book to prospective wholesalers or distributors or stores. Get these reproduced as cheaply as you can and in quantities that you think will be used fairly quickly. Depending on whether you design and prepare camera-ready copy, or whether you have a printer prepare the material for you, the cost per flyer will run between $0.08 and $0.25. Unless you have a sizeable budget, lots of time and energy, and an enormous list of places to send flyers, 1,000 is plenty. Smaller quantities leave more flexibility to modify brochures for particular audiences. Tailor these pieces toward these audiences—whether single buyer, library or bookstore.

You may find that you will have to write copy for inclusion in catalogs that will list your book. Catalog copy writing demands stating the crucial points about your book clearly and attractively in a limited number of words. While it takes time to do this, at least there is no charge for writing catalog copy.

Your book may be about a "hot" topic and therefore ripe for possible sale of excerpts to magazines, or for subsidiary or reprint rights, or a number of other exciting possibilities. This of course means hours spent mining the library for the appropriate names, publications and address, and the inevitable letter writing informing those people of the opportunity your book presents.

For some people, composing all the promotional material is an unpleasant task and very time consuming. You may want to consider hiring a media person or publicist for the contacts such a person may have in the media. A publicist may charge by the hour, at a rate ranging from $60 to $100 per hour. More commonly, the charge is based on the project. When you talk to a publicist, have some idea of just what it is you want and need. Be open to ideas and suggestions offered. Check larger local libraries for books listing media contacts (with contact people and addresses). Directories of radio and television stations, of newspapers (sorted by periodicity—daily, weekly, whatever—see Information Resources), magazines, associations and so forth exist and are veritable treasure troves.

When I published *Roughing It Elegantly*, I felt that since I had some background in newspaper writing, I could manage print promotion. However, I had no confidence in my ability to manage exposure on radio or television, so I hired a publicist. In addition to arranging an impressive array of appearances on local radio and television, she also prepared a news release announcing the book, as by the time I had gotten the book into production, I was fairly wrung dry of ideas, and had been too close to the book as well. Though the cost of the publicist came to about $2,000, I consider it a good investment.

To give you some notion of the money involved in getting the book into the world, by July 31, four months after the finished books arrived into my hands, I had spent $9,230. Books had begun to sell, though, and I had by then taken in $4,200.

Ongoing Promotion

Once your book is out, your efforts can't stop. You must rely on other ways you can keep your book in booksellers' minds and in the public's eye. Some ways cost money; others merely take time (particularly if you are faithful in following up on letters you have sent out).

Advertising is one way to keep sales up. Place ads in your distributors' catalogs and periodicals. This can get quite expensive ($150 a pop for the smallest sized ad), and may or may not be effective. Advertise in publications that pertain to your book's subject area. However, unless you have several books, or an extremely timely or particularly useful subject, this is probably not a good way to go, either.

Another way, with a wide range of cost, is through exhibitions. Exhibiting your book at trade shows like those of the American Booksellers Association or the American Library Association or the regional and state associations is a useful way of promoting your book. After all, nothing beats having the book in plain view for potential buyers. For most single book publishers, it is not economically feasible to take a booth at the large national shows, but it may be worthwhile to do so at regional trade shows. Consider sharing booth costs and space with another publisher, though. The national publishers organizations also provide opportunity to their members to display at a fairly modest cost. (See Addresses for listings of national and regional associations.)

Don't overlook the non-book trade shows related to your book's field. If your book is about electronics, investigate the possibility of selling your book at electronics shows. Janet Martin, who writes humorous books about Scandinavian characters, has sold many copies of her books at the various ethnic festivals around the Upper Midwest.

Small publishers can exhibit fairly inexpensively at some local festivals. Arrange to have a book-signing at a local bookstore. Be prepared to help promote the event vigorously.

Investigate other means of promotion. Books don't promote themselves, and rarely do they develop legs except yours. One way to promote your book is to teach a class, with or without your book as a text. In fact, the teaching of a class is often a reason for producing a book, as Pat Dorff (*File, Don't Pile*™) found out. This book too grew out of classes I taught.

Make yourself interesting and available to local media people, particularly for radio and television. On one hand, they are besieged with people wanting to get on the air. On the other hand, they are always in desperate need of good material for their programs.

Public speaking, if you enjoy or don't mind it, is an excellent way to promote a book. Develop a talk based on useful or fun parts of your book, and then hunt out groups that would like to hear what you have to say. A slide show based on material in your book or relating to it is a nice option. Some authors find that they can do quite nicely, thank you, with a tiny or no speaking fee if they can sell their books afterward.

Or, if you are so inclined, write articles drawn from your book. This is easier said than done. Getting paid for these pieces is nice, too.

You will need to do a good bit of research to find the appropriate spots for your pieces, and then you will need to interest editors in purchasing them.

Finally, your own alert observation and inventiveness may show you opportunities to promote your book. You did, after all, write a book in the field.

8

To Publish or Not To Publish

IF you want your book published, you have read about two options. You can continue the hunt for a publisher, or you can publish it yourself. Only you can decide whether you have the wherewithal, with emphasis on the *all*, to do the job yourself. Rejection by publisher after publisher is difficult to take, and you may come to believe, rightly or wrongly, that there is no place for your book. (Now, after reading this book, you may have a little better idea *why* publishers decide not to publish a book. They are interested in not only recovering their investment but in making a profit as well.)

It may very well be that after you have read this book, you may decide that consigning your manuscript to the Bottom Desk Drawer or the Round File is the wisest course of action. If you decide to publish, you will spend enormous amounts of time learning what you need to know to publish a book; you will spend equally enormous amounts of time doing the things you learned that should be done; you will spend money—enough to buy a car—to produce the book and to get it into the marketplace. You may decide that publishing your own book isn't your cup of tea.

The odds of a book appearing in print and selling are rather like the odds of a single acorn growing into a splendid mature oak. A single tree will produce thousands, some of which become food for squirrels and birds; most eventually rot. Yet you know very well that some of the acorns *do* grow into trees.

Do You Want *to Become a Publisher?*

If you have read this far, you know that there is not only a great deal to learn (and that is a never-ending process), but that there are substantial risks to be undertaken. You will invest money, with no sure promise of return. To be sure, you can do a great deal to minimize those risks and assure a reasonable return on your investment. You will invest emotional as well as physical energy, with the risk of hurt and disappointment. Yet the real bottom line is whether the prospect of actually being a publisher is sufficiently attractive for you to put out the time and money.

What's Next?

If you publish your book, and hence become a publisher, what would you do for an encore? Will your book warrant later revision and updating, hence republication? Is there a second book that can follow this one? You can't expect it to perform the same way as the first, either. Is there one after that? It is difficult to interest book dealers (wholesale, retail, etc.) in buying a single title. It looks lonesome. It looks like you are not serious about publishing.

Becoming a publisher involves an enormous amount of learning, a fair amount of expense, and a whale of a lot of work. You go through a great deal of effort with one book, laying groundwork for publicity and promotion, for distribution and sale for one title. With all that goes into publishing just one book, it is a shame to quit then. It's a little like the comment made about having a second child: since the first one takes *all* your time, a second one can't take any more.

If your book falls into certain categories, you can possibly expect it to have a life of perhaps three to five years. Do you want to have this one project be your primary project for that length of time, or do you want to go on to a new one?

Enhance Your Chances of Success

If you publish, will your book be "successful"? That is, what chances do you have for its intended public to buy and read it? What will be its life expectancy? Assuming that you have done a decent to fine job on writing the book, and that the finished product is well done, what will help it find its spot?

Your chances are greatly enhanced if you have a fresh, appealing topic. The independent publisher often is the first to see a niche for unique subject matter and fill it. Some have found their books so well received by the public that larger publishers have bought the rights to publish them. This happened to John Louis Anderson (the author of *Scandinavian Humor and Other Myths,*) and Ken Blanchard (*The One-Minute Manager*), to name a couple.

An enormous audience for a topic helps. People eat, and consequently cookbooks are always popular. Cookbooks also are examples for the specialized niches. Any day now we might expect something like *Ancient Mayan Cuisine*, and the odds are that if the book were interestingly written and well produced, it would sell.

Check the competition. How many books on your topic are in print? How many of them are in bookstores? How is yours going to be different and better? Don't check just the big chain stores; they specialize in rapidly moving titles. Look into several good independent bookstores, and especially look for the store that will be most likely to deal with that subject. Don't forget the nontraditional booksellers, either.

You Can Make It

Having told you about so many of the difficulties you can encounter, I should not leave you with the idea that publishing your own book is too great a task. While it *does* involve a huge amount of time and a considerable chunk of money, there is no good reason (aside from a total lack of funds) why you cannot boldly venture into publishing. Help is at hand. Important resources can be tapped; there is a sizable library of books on the various aspects of the whole project. Study diligently, using the resources suggested in this book. Make the numerous calculations, then double-check them. Consider whether your financial resources are up to the venture, and whether you do indeed have a good chance of getting back all your investment and more. (Your time should be worth something as well.)

Remember, too, the human resources available, either individuals or members of a publishers' group. I cannot overemphasize this. The assistance and support I got from members of the group I belong to was extraordinarily valuable. Talk to people who have published their own books. You will generally find that they are helpful to others who are thinking of following their example. (Do be considerate of their time; remember that time is one of their more important assets, and you shouldn't waste it.) Talk to people who can guide you to other important information sources. When (and if) you publish your book, acknowledge those who have helped you. (Send those people a copy of your book, signed with a thank you.) Later, when you are in a position to help someone else, remember the aid and comfort you received.

Think about the possible and probable effects publication will have on your life, and whether you like the prospects. The whole focus for a major portion of my life shifted after I published my first book. One, my time was greatly occupied with the whole business. Two, I knew I would revise *Roughing It Elegantly* in a few years, and that colored my approach to a favorite leisure-time activity and our vacations. Finally, publishing directed me into a totally new professional and social group, with a host of new friends.

There is no doubt about it; publishing a book *will* change your life, sometimes delightfully so, sometimes not. Equipped with the resources you find here and others that you will find as you pursue the issue, you can make a decision that is right for you. Publishing is a great adventure. Is it for you?

Recommended Reading

Many companies have produced a tremendous amount of material on subjects helpful to a novice publisher. This list is by no means comprehensive. Annotations are based on personal knowledge and recommendations from other publishers. Publication prices are given where known and appropriate.

A one-stop place for finding many useful books for the self-publisher, particularly the novice, is Ad-Lib Publications, 51½ West Adams, Fairfield, IA 52556. Write for their Recommended Books Order Form.

Trade Information

Huenefeld Report. The Huenefeld Company, Inc., P. O. Box 665, Bedford, MA 01730.

The emphasis of this newsletter is on what happens inside the publishing world. This is the place to learn about the economics of book publication, particularly in the smaller press world. Periodically, reports are made from respondent publishers on pay scales, print runs, production costs, etc. Year's subscription (26 issues) $88.

Coser, Lewis A., Charles Kadushin; and Walter W. Powell. *Books: The Culture and the Commerce of Publishing,* University of Chicago Press, Chicago, IL. 1985. $12.50.

Dessauer, John. *Book Publishing,* R. R. Bowker, New York, NY. 1981, $29.95 (cloth); $15.95 (paper).

Kaufmann, William F. *One Book/Five Ways.* 1978. $19.95 (cloth); $12.95 (paper).

Set of case studies, based on a hypothetical book as handled by five different publishers.

Publishers Weekly. Cahners Publishing Company; Publishers Weekly, 249 West 17th Street, New York, NY 10011.

This weekly magazine, the primary periodical publication to the trade, chronicles book trade activities, changes of personnel (major editors, owners, etc.), new books, trends in the bookselling world. Year's subscription $119.

Shatzkin, Leonard. *In Cold Type—Overcoming the Book Crisis,* Houghton Mifflin. 1983. $8.95 (paper).

Literary Market Place. R. R. Bowker, New York.

This annual has sections listing book publishers, editorial Services and agents, electronic publishing, paper merchandising and other services and supplies. Useful for surveying the whole scene, but should be augmented by seeking out what is available in your area.

Writing

Bunnin, Brad. *The Writer's Loyal Companion.* Addison-Wesley Publishing, Reading, MA. 1988.

Maggio, Rosalie. *How to Say It: Choice Words, Phrases, Sentences & Paragraphs for Every Situation.* Prentice Hall, Englewood Cliffs, NJ. 1990. $14.95 (paper).

Handy reference for composing of a wide range of business letters, filled with graceful yet appropriate phrasing.

Editing

Chicago Guide to Preparing Electronic MS for Authors and Publishers. University of Chicago Press, Chicago, IL. 1987.

Directory of Freelance Editors, Writers, and Proofreaders. Professional Editors Network (PEN), P. O. Box 19265, Minneapolis, MN 55419-0265.

Strunk, William, Jr., and E. B. White. *The Elements of Style,* Macmillan, New York. Third Edition, 1979.

This is classic and important for "writing it right."

Zinsser, William K. *On Writing Well: An Informal Guide to Writing Non-fiction.* Harper & Row, New York, NY. Second Edition, 1980.

Useful for self-editing; the author gives examples from his own work.

Also get one of several style sheets, such as the

A Manual of Style, for Authors, Editors, and Copywriters (also known as the *Chicago Style Book*), University of Chicago Press, Chicago, IL. $37.50.

Get this stylebook, or the *MLA* (Modern Language Association) *Handbook, for Writers of Research Papers, Theses, and Dissertations*, or the *Los Angeles Times Stylebook: a Manual for Writers, Editors, Journalists and Students*. Faithfully following a stylebook also insures consistency of form throughout. Use it to learn the correct ways of preparing your manuscript—proper use of italics, getting permissions for use of material, paragraphing, organization of a book's front matter, typesetting, the whole works.

The *MLA Handbook* is *the* reference for academic work.

Don't overlook the basic reference books, including a dictionary and a thesaurus.

Publishing

Appelbaum, Judith. *How to Get Happily Published*. Harper & Row, NY. 1988. $18.95 (case).

Get the revised edition, not the earlier one with Evans. This points more toward having someone else publish your book, but does touch on self-publishing. Its particular strong points are the proper way to prepare a manuscript and what publishers look for.

Balkin, Richard. *A Writer's Guide to Book Publishing*. Hawthorn/ Dutton, NY. 1981. $9.25 (paper).

Balkin, among other things, talks about how publishers go about marketing a book, valuable and useful information for the self-publisher.

Both Appelbaum's and Balkin's books have an excellent index, which should tell you something to do about your own non-fiction book.

Bodian, Nat. *Bodian's Publication Desk*. Oryx Press, Phoenix, AZ. 1988.

Boswell, John. *The Awful Truth About Publishing: Why They Always Reject Your Manuscript...& What You Can do About It*. Warner Books, NY. 1986.

Henderson, Bill. *The Publish-It-Yourself Handbook*. Harper & Row, New York, NY. 1987.

One of the first in the field, it is still highly regarded.

Huenefeld, John. *Huenefeld Guide To Book Publishing*. Mills & Sanderson, Box 665, Bedford, MA. $29.95.

Important book for understanding how the publishing industry works, and basic for the business side of it.

Mwadilifu, Dr. Mwalimu I. *How to Publish and Market Your Own Book as an Independent African Heritage Book Publisher.* ECA Associates Press, P. O. Box 15004, Chesapeake, VA 23320. $14.95.

Pitzer, Sara. *How to Write a Cook Book & Get it Published.* Writer's Digest Books, 9933 Alliance Road, Cincinnati, OH. 1984. $15.95 (case).

Excellent for anyone considering producing a cookbook. Pitzer tosses in several useful tidbits about actual costs, more so than Poynter or Ross.

Poynter, Dan. *The Self-Publishing Manual* (6th edition). Para Publishing, P. O. Box 4232, Santa Barbara, CA 93140-4232. $19.95 (paper).

This book is invaluable. Poynter takes the novices by the hand and leads them right through the publishing process. Used in conjunction with the Rosses' book *The Complete Guide to Self-Publishing*, one can go right down the line and do what has to be done. Best of all, Poynter has lists, lists, and lists of useful and pertinent information. In earlier editions, the index was a case in point for having a professional do the job, rather than a computer program. The index has been improved in later editions.

—. *Publishing Short-Run Books.* Para Publishing, P. O. Box 4232, Santa Barbara, CA 93140-4232. $5.95 (paper).

Offers a great many useful tips on doing all the production work (short of actual printing).

—. *Publishing Forms.* Para Publishing, P. O. Box 4232, Santa Barbara, CA 93140-4232. $14.95 (paper) and several others. He also has a helpful newsletter. Ordering one of his books gets you on the list to receive the newsletter.

—. Special reports on book publishing.

Poynter has an extensive series of reports on specific topics: book marketing, book reviews, news releases, direct mail advertising, selling books abroad, and credit cards, to name a few. These are *reports,* not books, ranging from 10 to 61 pages.

Poynter has established a solid position as an authoritative voice on self-publishing, and he zealously guards the position by keeping his materials thoroughly current, a point would-be

publishers should note.

Poynter, Dan, and Mindy Bingham. *Is There a Book Inside You? How to Successfully Author a Book Alone or Through Collaboration* (revised). Para Publishing, P. O. Box 4232, Santa Barbara, CA 93140-4232. 1987. $9.95 (paper).

Whether there is a book that should be published or not is addressed in this book. The chapter, "Your Publishing Options," is excellent in its succinct description of the choices available in publishing a book.

Ross, Marilyn and Tom. *The Complete Guide to Self-Publishing.* Writer's Digest Books, Cincinnati, OH. 1985. $19.95 (cloth).

Writer's Digest Books has an extensive library of books for the writer and would-be publisher. This one is regarded as a classic and is basic for the would-be self-publisher. There is some overlap with Poynter's book, but the lists supplied include names Poynter doesn't, and vice versa. Good index.

All the above books have extensive reference sections, according to category, and are well worth having for the resources they outline.

West, Celeste. *The Passionate Perils of Publishing,* Booklegger Press, 555 29th Street, San Francisco, CA. 1980.

Business Planning

Cook, James R. *The Start-Up Entrepreneur.* E. P. Dutton, New York, NY. 1989. $18.95.

This book takes a look at business basics and the emotional and inspirational drives of the entrepreneur.

Mancuso, Joseph R. *How to Prepare and Present a Business Plan.* Prentice-Hall Press, NY. 1991. $11.

McKeever, Mike. *How to Write a Business Plan.* Nolo Press. $14.

This book is described as having great detail on all the elements and benefits of business and cites other books as resources. It appears to be quite useful and the price is reasonable.

Pinson, Linda & Jerry Jinnett. *Anatomy of A Business Plan.* Out of Your Mind...And Into The Marketplace, 13381 White Sand Drive, Tustin, CA. 1989. $24 (paper).

Shaffer, Charles A., Madeline Harris and Mary J. Kruger, eds. *A Guide to Starting a Business in Minnesota.* Minnesota Small

Business Assistance Office, 900 American Center Building, 150 East Kellogg Boulevard, St. Paul, MN 55101. This guide is updated annually. Check your own state's Small Business Office for comparable publications.

Write for free copy. An absolute must.

Starting and Managing a Business From Your Home. Department 146R, Consumer Information Center, Pueblo, CO. $1.75.

Superintendent of Documents. *Starting and Managing A Small Business of Your Own.* (SBA 1.15:1/4), U.S. Government Printing Office, Washington, DC 20402.

Startup: An Entrepreneur's Guide to Launching and Managing a New Venture. Rock Beach Press, 1255 University Avenue, Rochester, NY 14607. 1989.

Production

Beach, Mark, Steve Shepro and Ken Russon. *Getting It Printed: How to Work With Printers and Graphic Arts Services to Assure Quality, Stay on Schedule, and Control Costs.* Coast to Coast Books, 1115 SE Stephens Street, Portland, OR 97214. 1986. $29.50 (paper), $40 (cloth).

ComputerEdge staff. *How to Get Started in Desktop Publishing.* Computer Publishing Enterprises, P. O. Box 23478, San Diego, CA 92123. 1990. $7.95 (paper).

Fenton, Erfert. *The Macintosh Font Book: Typographic Tips, Techniques, and Resources.* Peachpit Press, Berkeley, CA. 2nd edition 1991. $23.95 (paper).

If you are thinking of designing your own book, this is a fine starting place, with its abundant examples of typefaces and helpful discussions of why not to use certain typefaces in particular applications. The Appendices offer informative material on alternate typeface names as used by various computer typemakers. Strongly recommended for its information and for its clarity of presentation.

Kremer, John. *Directory of Book Printers 1992 Edition.* Open Horizons, P.O. Box 205, Fairfield, IA 52556-0205. $9.95 (paper).

Very useful on general matter of buying printing. The original version of this book, *Directory of Short-Run Book Printers*, has been superseded and expanded into the present volume. It is not a substitute for shopping the print market in your particular area, but it does give comments from other small publishers on their experiences with various printers.

Poynter, Dan. *Publishing Short-Run Books.* Para Publishing, P.O. Box 4232, Santa Barbara, CA 93140-4232. 4th edition 1987. $5.95 (paper).

Detailed instruction on how to put together an ultra-short run of books without it costing an arm and a leg.

Publisher's Planning Kit.. Delta Lithograph Company. 14731 California Street, Van Nuys, CA 91411.

This is not a book but an excellent kit that identifies the questions that should be asked about putting a book into production, especially when talking with the printer. Write and request.

Swann, Alan. *How to Understand and Use Design and Layout.* North Light Books, 1507 Dana Avenue, Cincinnati, OH. 1987

Highly recommended by those who design and lay out books.

The Twin Cities Gold Book. Prime Publications, Inc., 318 Groveland, Minneapolis, MN 55403. $16.95. 798 pp.

An annual publication, *The Gold Book* is a "spectrum directory," in that it lists 5,000 companies in 53 categories covering the advertising, publishing, communications and creative services (graphic design, animation, etc.) industries in the metro Minneapolis-St. Paul area. Prime Publications produces a similar book for Phoenix, Arizona. If your library does not have this book, ask your librarian what spectrum directories might be available in your area.

Twin Cities Creative Sourcebook. MAXAM Group, Inc., 401 North Third Street, Suite 400, Minneapolis, MN 55401.

A compilation of "the best creative talent in Minnesota." Features illustration, photography, design, film and video production and other related services. This would be a good starting point to educate yourself on the artwork you would be contending with in designing a book, producing its brochures, etc. Similar books in other communities are *Chicago Talent Sourcebook* and the *California Workbook.* MAXAM Publishing, Inc., 450 Alabama Street, Suite 100, San Francisco, California 94110, also publishes the *Bay Area Creative Sourcebook.* Check your local library.

Will-Harris, Daniel. *TypeStyle: How to Choose and Use Type on a*

Personal Computer. Peachpit Press, Berkeley, CA. 1990. $24.95 (paper).

At $24.95, this is a fairly expensive paperback, but I would say without hesitation that it is well worth the money, particularly if you decide to produce the layout for your own book. The book abounds with examples of all sorts of type and discussions about their effectiveness. Reading it is an essential before working with a typesetter for your book. Better still, get your own copy.

Williams, Robin. *The Mac Is Not a Typewriter.* Peachpit Press, Berkeley, CA. 1990. $9.95 (paper).

For the newcomer to the Macintosh computer, Williams provides numerous tips for producing better-looking print with technique tips that overcome that high school Typing I class.

—. *The PC Is Not a Typewriter.* Peachpit Press, Berkeley, CA. 1991. $9.95 (paper).

Williams has produced a corresponding book for IBM and IBM-compatible computers.

—. *The Little Mac Book.* Peachpit Press, Berkeley, CA. 2nd edition 1991. $12.95 (paper).

One of the best beginner's books on using a computer and its word-processing capabilities I have seen. Would that the computer manual writers could write so clearly and helpfully!

Marketing

Ballou, Melinda-Carol, Marie Keifer and John Kremer. *Specialty Booksellers Directory.* Ad-Lib Publications, 51½ West Adams, Fairfield, IA 52556. $19.95 (paper). 1987.

Since booksellers are listed alphabetically, then sorted by specialty, and cross-referenced by state, this is a useful item for direct mailing to stores. Mailing labels according to category are also available from Ad-Lib. The information tends to get out of date: bookselling is a tough business, and many stores do not survive.

Bodian, Nat. G. *Marketing Handbook: Tips and Techniques for the Sale and Promotion of Scientific, Technical, Professional, and Scholarly Books and Journals.* R. R. Bowker, New York, NY. 1980.

—. *Copywriter's Handbook: A Practical Guide for Advertising and Promotion of Specialized and Scholarly Books and Journals.* ISI

Press, Philadelphia, PA. 1984. $19.95 (paper).

Bodian is considered a major guru in the field of direct mail marketing. Direct mail selling is a very different breed of cat from bookstore selling. If you are thinking of marketing your books by direct mail, you would be well advised to do a lot of study. Direct mail marketing means working on a sizeable scale, and you had better have the financial and personnel resources to get into it.

Carter, Robert A., ed. *Trade Book Marketing: A Practical Guide.* R.R. Bowker, New York, NY. 1983.

The Great Catalog Guide. Direct Marketing Association, Inc., 6 East 43rd Street, New York, NY 10017.

Booklet of more than 600 catalogs, addresses and areas of specialty. $2.

Kremer, John. *Book Marketing Made Easier, 3rd Edition.* Ad-Lib Publications, 51½ West Adams, Fairfield, IA 52556. $19.95 (paper).

This is an excellent book for the beginner to get even before deciding to self-publish, as it lays out virtually all the things that have to be done for marketing a book, even to providing sample forms ("Formaides") for getting your book listed in the places it needs to be listed. Includes worksheets for marketing plans, etc. Recommended.

—. *1001 Ways To Market Your Books—For Publishers and Authors.* 1989. Ad-Lib Publications, 51½ West Adams, Fairfield, IA 52556. $14.95 (paper), $19.95 (cloth). 1990.

Get this most thorough book *before* you start to publish. From fundamentals of marketing, to book design as an adjunct to sales, to defining your market, advertising and finding ways to promote your book, Kremer covers it all with practical and useful tips. Well worth the money.

Manning, Matthew, Fay Shapiro, and Frank Renkiewicz, eds. *The National Directory of Catalogs.* Oxbridge Communications, Inc., 150 Fifth Avenue, New York, NY 10011. $145.00 (paper).

An annual directory and excellent source of information on companies producing catalogs, their areas of interest, size and frequency of publication, etc. Lists 4,022 U.S. and Canadian catalogs. Look here for places to place your book(s).

Pinson, Linda, and Jerry Jinnett. *Marketing: Researching & Reaching Your Target Market.* Out of Your Mind...And Into The

Marketplace, 13381 White Sand Drive, Tustin, CA 92680. $22. (paper)

I haven't read this, but a colleague recommended it.

Playle, Ron. *Selling to Catalog Houses.* Playle Publications, Inc., P. O. Box 775, Des Moines, IA 50303.

Booklet; also available, 200 major mail order houses on labels for $15.

Powers, Melvin. *How to Self-Publish Your Book & Have The Fun & Excitement of Being A Best-Selling Author.* 1984. Wilshire Book Company, 12015 Sherman Road, North Hollywood, CA 91605. $10 (paper).

This book was designed and written to be sold through direct marketing. Author also wrote *How to Get Rich in Mail Order = $2 million.*

Promotion

Poynter, Dan. *Book Fairs.* Para Publishing, P. O. Box 4232, Santa Barbara, CA 93140-4232.

Worth looking into. Independent publishers tend to underutilize book fairs.

Also, Poynter rents his mailing lists. The prices are modest and he works diligently to keep his lists clean and up to date. Categories include special interest magazines, book reviewers, radio and television, the writing business, and the book publishing business.

Technical Support

Gookin, Dan. *How to Understand and Buy Computers.* Computer Publishing Enterprises, P. O. Box 23478, San Diego, CA 92123. 1991. $7.95 (paper).

Wang, Wally. *How to Understand and Find Software.* Computer Publishing Enterprises, P. O. Box 23478, San Diego, CA 92123. 1989. $7.95 (paper).

Periodicals

Book Marketing Update. Formerly published by Ad-Lib Publications, now published by Open Horizons Company, P O Box

205, Fairfield, IA 52556-0205. Monthly publication, $48 per year.

Edited by the indefatigable John Kremer, this is one publication that should not be thrown away at the end of a month or two. It is also becoming an excellent forum for information and idea sharing among independent publishers.

Book Promotion Hotline. Published weekly by Ad-Lib Publications, 51½ West Adams, Fairfield, IA 52556. $150.00 per year.

Another of John Kremer's productions.

Entrepreneur, The Small Business Authority. Entrepreneur, Inc., 2392 Morse Avenue, Irvine, CA 92714. Monthly publication, $19.97 per year.

Standing features include Trend Watch, Advertising Workshop, Off The Shelf (books), Management Tools, features on taxes, computers for business, issues affecting your business, and others.

Home-Office Computing. published monthly by Scholastic, Inc., 730 Broadway, New York, NY 10003. Monthly publication, $19.97 per year.

Major topics covered in include computing, desk-top publishing, software, running a mail-order business (May 1990), finance, telecomputing, business (e.g., Should You Charge More For Your Services? (May 1990)).

Library Journal. Cahners Publishing Company, 249 West 17th Street, New York, NY 10011.

Monthly publication aimed at the librarian, with updates on new books, reviews.

School Library Journal, published monthly by Cahners Publishing Company 249 West 17th Street, New York, NY 10011.

The *Library Journal* for schools.

Information Resources

Print Research Sources

Publishers should be particularly aware of the following publications, as they are published to the industry. THESE ARE IMPORTANT!

Book Publishers of The United States & Canada. *Contemporary Authors.*

R. R. Bowker: publishes directories and reference books used by decision-makers in the library, bookselling, communications and publishing worlds.

American Book Trade Directory. Lists more than 19,000 book outlets in North America, plus listings of wholesalers and distributors.

AV Market Place, On Cassette (audiocassettes)

Books in Print. Bowker claims *BIP* has over 1,000,000 entries.

Bowker Annual of American Library Directory.

Bowker's Legal Publishing Preview

Forthcoming Books. FB anticipates, according to Bowker, up to 5,000 titles five months in advance. About 10 percent may be reviewed in *Publishers Weekly.*

International Literary Market Place

Literary Market Place

Publisher's Trade List Annual

Software Encyclopedia

Cahners Publishing Company. *Publisher's Trade List Annual*

Dustbooks. *International Directory of Little Magazines and Small Presses.*

Gale Research Company. Gale Research Tower, Detroit, MI

Encyclopedia of Associations. Lists over 20,000 associations in the U.S. and other countries. Identifies key people, provides address, phone number, publication, if any, staff and budget size, and other pertinent information.

Directory of Directories. Comprehensive list of directories, as name implies.

Directory of Publications. Lists, as implied, publications in U. S. and Canada. Identifies by periodicity (weekly, monthly, daily, etc.,) size of circulation, key editors, with usual info of address and phone number.

Organizations Master Index.

Hudson's Newsletter Directory. 44 West Market Street, P. O. Box 311, Rhinebeck, NY 12572. $99.

H. W. Wilson. *Cumulative Book Index, A World List of Books in the English Language.* H. W. Wilson, 950 University Avenue, New York, NY 10452.

Electronic Databases

People who live near a public library that provides a wide and deep range of services have a treasure available. A huge portion of the population, though, is not able to drop into one of these libraries. A computer and modem makes it possible to tap into information networks for the price of a long-distance phone call, no matter where one lives.

Often an author is not in a good position to do the actual research to turn up necessary data. What you as author or potential publisher should know is there are numerous electronic networks enabling you to tap into an incredible amount of information. Tapping into those networks usually involves a fee, but the desired information will be well worth it. Library systems will generally have some sort of network, if you can find out what it is.

Not surprisingly, there are people who make it their business to come up with those valuable nuggets of information, often on a free-lance basis. The key words to use in finding out who you want to know is *Information specialist* or *information broker.* Information specialists or brokers may be librarians by training who like the hunt for information and know how to rummage through the appropriate publications and particularly to mine the on-line databases that are major lodes of information. Since it takes one to know one, ask your librarian about information specialists in your area. Fees (ranging from $35 to $80 per hour) may seem high, but if you know what you want to find out, the desired material may emerge in an hour or less. As with other service providers we've discussed, you are paying not only for the expertise they have, but the time you don't have to spend on something you may not be particularly adept at.

Nationally, there is the Association of Independent Information Professionals (formerly the International Association of Independent Information Brokers). Information brokers are also listed in the more or less annual *Directory of Fee-Based Informational Services* (Houston, Burrell Enterprises).

For the computer buffs, several on-line information sources, such as The Source, CompuServe, Prodigy, and others, also provide access to staggering quantities of information. An information broker also reminded me that Dialog (especially with its Knowledge Index) and Datatimes are valuable to the information seeker. A library can provide phone numbers (usually 800 numbers) for contacting these services to get a brochure.

More and more large library systems are going on-line with their catalogs and specialized databases. It is well worth the time to learn how to use these computer-stored resources.

Organizations

It is useful to know how to find specialty people, especially if you don't live in a metropolitan area.

American Society of Indexers, Inc., 1700 18th Street, N. W., Washington, DC 20009. They maintain a register of indexers available for free-lance work. Write to inquire for your area.

Association of Independent Information Professionals, 801 Arch Street, Philadelphia, PA 19107.

Freelance Editorial Association. P. O. Box 835, Cambridge, MA 02238. Members are editors, writers, proofreaders, indexers, translators, project managers and desktop publishing specialists.

Service Corps of Retired Executives (SCORE), 409 Third Street S.W., Suite 5900, Washington, DC 20024 (202/205-6762). Experience trains great teachers. This organization, composed of people who have worked in businesses, provides assistance to small business owners, both new and existing. Local chapters hold seminars or workshops addressed to particular concerns, and the beauty part is that the services are free. Write for contacts in your area.

Publicity Contacts

These are library materials—useful, but not often enough for the beginning publisher to warrant buying them immediately.

Bacon's Publicity Checker.

Benn's Media Directory. Comprehensive, 2-volume work also includes International and United Kingdom media listings.

1990 Media Encyclopedia: Working Press of the Nation (4 vol.)

Broadcasting Yearbook. This lists National Associations and Professional Societies, too.

International Year Book of Editor & Publisher.

Gale Directory of Publications and Broadcast Media. Gale Research. Formerly *Ayer's Directory.* Annual; state by state, alphabetical list, with address, phone and fax numbers, purpose of the publication, frequency of publication, key personnel, and circulation figures. Very useful.

Publishers Directory, Thomas M. Bachman, ed. (Gale Research)

Oxbridge Communications, Inc., 150 Fifth Avenue, Suite 636, New York, New York 10011, also publishes

Standard Periodical Directory. Lists over 75,000 U.S. and Canadian periodicals published by any field, subject or industry. $395.

Oxbridge Directory of Newsletters. Lists 19,500 U.S. and Canadian newsletters in 168 subject categories, indexed by title. Annual. $245.

National Directory of Magazines. Lists information on publication, staff, advertising and list rates, circulation size, and production information. Valuable for marketers and public relations people. $225.

Ulrich's International Periodical Directory. 3 volumes. Material here is arranged by subject, with index by title. A particularly useful distinction for *Ulrich's* is that it lists periodicals which have ceased publication.

Addresses

Book Numbers

ISBN (ISSN for magazines) assignment

ISBN Agency (U.S.), R.R. Bowker, 121 Chanlon Road, New Providence, NJ 07974. (908/665-6770)

A new publisher should write a letter on his or her letterhead requesting ISBN assignment.

Library of Congress Catalog Card number preassignment

Library of Congress, Cataloging in Publication Division, Washington, DC 20540.

You will receive the appropriate form and a kit describing the Cataloging in Publication procedures.

Copyright information

U. S. Copyright Office, Library of Congress, Washington, DC. 20559.

For books or other print work, ask for Form TX. File for the copyright registration after the publication of your book. Circular R1, Copyright Basics, spells it all out.

Organizations

National Publishers or Trade Organizations
Association of American Publishers, Inc.
220 East 23rd Street
New York, NY 10010-4686

COSMEP: The International Association of Independent Publishers
P.O. Box 703
San Francisco, CA 94101

Evangelical Christian Publishers Association
950 West Southern, Suite 106-B
Tempe, AZ 83282

Multicultural Publishers Exchange
P.O. Box 9869
Madison, WI 53715

National Association of Independent Publishers
P.O. Box 430
Highland City, FL 33846-0430

NAPRA (New Age Publishing & Retailing Alliance)
P.O. Box 9
Eastsound, WA 98245

Independent Publishers Associations

Regional as well as state or area groups are listed. Addresses of these groups will vary according to the current president. Since they are volunteer organizations, most do not have an executive officer and permanent address. There are doubtless others.

Baltimore Publishers Association
P.O. Box 5584
Baltimore, MD 21285-5584

Book Publishers Northwest
P.O. Box 22048
Seattle, WA 98122

Florida Publishers Group
P.O. Box 262261
Tampa, FL 33685

Maine Writers & Publishers
12 Pleasant Street
Brunswick, ME 04011

Marin Small Publishers Association
P.O. Box 1346
Ross, CA 94957

Michigan Publishers Association
Lawells Publishing
P.O. Box 1338
Royal Oak, MI 48068-1338

Mid-America Publishers Association (MAPA)
P.O. Box 30242
Lincoln, NE 68503-0242

Midwest Independent Publishers Association (MIPA)
9561 Woodridge Circle
Eden Prairie, MN 55347-2744

Northwest Association of Book Publishers
P.O. Box 633
Marylhurst, OR 97036

Rocky Mountain Book Publishers Association
Alan Stark, Executive Director
P.O. Box 583
Niwot, CO 80544

Book Publishers of Texas Association
3404 South Ravinia Drive
Dallas, TX 75233

Tucson Book Publishing Association
P.O. Box 43542
Tucson, AZ 85733

Marketing Groups

Publishers Marketing Association
2401 Pacific Coast Highway, Suite #102
Hermosa Beach, CA 90254

Booksellers Organizations

American Booksellers Association (ABA)
828 South Broadway
Tarrytown, NY 10591

Christian Booksellers Association
P.O. Box 200
Colorado Springs, CO 80901

Association of Booksellers for Children
Caron Chapman
c/o Learn Me Books
175 Ash Street
St. Paul, MN 55126

Regional Booksellers Organizations

Many of these organizations have volunteer staffs; the addresses tend to change as new people take office.

Booksellers Association of Georgia
Rupert Le Craw, President
Oxford Books, Inc.
2345 Peachtree Road NE
Atlanta, GA 30305

Chesapeake Regional Area Booksellers Association
Maria Spencer, President
Parks & History Association
P.O. Box 40929
Washington, DC 20116

Gateway Booksellers Association
Gus Churchill
12750 Coachlight Square Drive
Florissant, MO 63033

Great Lakes Booksellers Association
Jim Dana, Executive Director
The Bookman
P.O. Box 901
Grand Haven, MI 49417

Houston Area Booksellers Association
Greg Newton, President
Sam Houston Bookshop
5015 Westheimer-Galleria #1450
Houston, TX 77056

Intermountain Booksellers Association
Linda Brummett, Past President
BYU Bookstore
Brigham Young University
Provo, UT 84602

Mid-Atlantic Booksellers Association
Larry Robin, President
Robin's Bookstore
108 South 13th Street
Philadelphia, PA 19107

Midwest Booksellers Association
Ellen Scott
The Bookhouse
3808 South 109th Street
Omaha, NE 68144

Mountains & Plains Booksellers Association
Lisa Knudsen, Executive Director
805 LaPorte Avenue
Fort Collins, CO 80521

New England Booksellers Association
Sharon Kirby, Executive Director
45 Newbury Street, #506
Boston, MA 02116

New Mexico Booksellers Association
Judith Walker, President
Corner Bookstore
3500 Central SE, #20C
Albuquerque, NM 87106

New Orleans/Gulf South Booksellers Association
Mark Zumpe, President
Maple Street Book Shops
P.O. Box 750043
New Orleans, LA 70118

New York/New Jersey Booksellers Association
Cyd Rosenberg
397 Arbuckle Avenue
Cedarhurst, NY 11516

Northern California Booksellers Association
Melissa Mytinger, Executive Director
2124 Kittredge Street, Box 1
Berkeley, CA 94704

Oklahoma Independent Booksellers Association
Jerry Brace, President
Brace Books & More
2205 North 14th
Ponca City, OK 74601

Pacific Northwest Booksellers Association
Bonny McKenney, Executive Director
5903 SE 19th Avenue
Portland, OR 97202

San Diego Booksellers Association
President
P.O. Box 1908
San Diego, CA 92112

Southeast Booksellers Association
Wanda Jewell, Executive Director
3806 Yale Avenue
Columbia, SC 29205

South-Central Booksellers Association
Julia Bentley, President
Memphis State University Bookstore
University Center
Memphis, TN 8152

Southern California Booksellers Association
Darcy Critchfield, Executive Coordinator
1223 Wilshire Boulevard, #526
Santa Monica, CA 90403

Southwestern Booksellers Association
Marvin C. Steakley, President
Southern Methodist University Bookstore
Box 8362
Dallas, TX 75205-0362

Upper Midwest Booksellers Association
Susan Walker, Executive Director
4018 West 65th Street
Edina, MN 55435

There are numerous regional special interests groups. Inquire from your regional association.

Computer Records for Publishers

Aside from a word-processing program for your computer, two other pieces of software are essential. (True, you could maintain all this by hand, but it is tedious, and does not lend itself well to extracting useful information.)

You need a spreadsheet program for calculating and general bookkeeping, and a database program for managing all manner of information that you will develop. Several good accounting packages are on the market, but they are dedicated programs—good for the accounting, and they are not cheap. Accountant, Inc., (Softsync, Inc.) is one such program. Setting it up will teach you a great deal about accounting. A basic spreadsheet is relatively inexpensive and can be made to do a wide variety of tasks.

Spreadsheet Records

The spreadsheet is used for a variety of records, including at the very least, cash flow, sales and payments, accounts, and tax information. You can create charts and graphs with several of the programs, useful for pictorial representation of what your company is doing.

General Cash Flow Ledger

A basic record that every business should maintain is the General Cash Flow ledger. This is an account of money that comes into (*Credit*) and goes out of (*Debit*) the business. You will need to identify the various categories these funds travel through, so they are set up in your General Cash Flow sheet. In addition to the Credit and Debit columns that record actual cash flow, the categories most frequently used are Promotion, Office supplies, Shipping costs Paid and Collected, Dues & Publications, Number of books sold, Discount applied, Total sale price of books sold, Sales tax received, Sales tax paid to the state, Bank Charges and Interest, Author's royalties (it's nice to keep track of what you as the author should be getting; it is a small measure of whether it was worth your time to write your book), Production, Capital investment, Research and development (for subsequent books), Phone calls, Contributions, and Miscellaneous. In time, you may add an employee or two, which you should list. The beauty of many spreadsheet programs is their flexibility—you can add categories as needed. Recently, I found that Intuit's program Quicken (Intuit) is useful for this sort of thing, and Quicken is a very inexpensive program. Careful study and patience will show you how to get more out of the program.

Total (paid) Sales	$8,003.94
Net Sales for year	$7,861.04

	Credit	Debit
Bank Credits	46.36	
Shipping Charged	47.57	
Sales Tax collected on sales	2.03	
Miscellaneous Credits	67.75	
Borrowed Capital	127.99	
Promotion		541.45
Office supplies		80.80
Shipping costs		150.10
Dues, Publications		327.00
Production		3,085.20
Research		0.00
Development		22.31
Capital items		3,145.00
Bank charges		177.15
Telephone calls		0.00
Contributions		0.00
Repairs		10.55
Royalties paid		0.00
Sales Tax to State		6.00
Returns		142.90
Travel		0.00
Miscellaneous		**5.00**
Totals	$8,295.64	$7,693.46
Balance		$602.18
Royalties due		$1,547.80

Cash Ledger Summary

A spreadsheet with the above categories (many with debit and credit columns of their own) gets wide. For that reason, I have a summary table of all categories of receipts and expenditures below the initial entry columns. Here, each category is listed, with income and expense columns, keyed to the column entry. Thus you have at a glance where your money comes from and where it goes. (See Cash Ledger Summary below.) While Quicken does not have such a summary table, it is fairly simple to generate a report that provides the desired information.

A trick I use is to set a cross-check table comparing the Credit/ Debit balance and the balance from the summary sheet. In it, I repeat the totals from the Cash Credit and Debit columns and get the balance. Alongside, I repeat the totals from the Summary Sheet. The discrepancy cell (I mark it so) of the cross-check is the difference between the balances. It makes life much simpler in the long run to locate and correct errors as they occur. Otherwise, you can spend *hours* trying to find the discrepancy.

General Book Sale Sheet

A second essential ledger is the General Book Sale sheet, where all book sales are recorded. (See General Sales Ledger Headings below.) In this spreadsheet, record (a) date and (b) buyer for each sale, (c) number of copies ordered, (d) discount, (e) discounted price total, (f) shipping charge, (g) sales tax (if applicable), and (h) total due. When payment has been made, record (i) amount paid and (j) date paid. Most orders are not prepaid. Since sales tax must be collected on books sold neither for resale nor to tax-exempt organizations (libraries and schools, for instance), you must track and report on your sales. The state generally is interested in gross sales, sales for resale, tax-exempt sales and interstate commerce. I habitually list the state with the purchaser's name when I have listed orders. I did so because I was interested in tracking where orders came from, but the practice is particularly useful if at some future point we are required to pay sales tax to states those purchasers buy from.

Date	Buyer	#	discount	Amt	Shipping	Total	Sales	Paid	Date pd
(a)	(b)	(c)	(d)	(e)	(f)	(g)	(h)	(i)	(j)

St resale	St exempt	St Indiv	OS resale	OS exempt	OS indiv
(k)	(l)	(m)	(n)	(o)	(p)

General Sales Ledger Headings

I also find it pertinent to list the invoice number I attach to each order. This simplifies tracking down the reference if needed by a distributor or wholesaler. A column for state of order could be added to the categories following.

Since I am also interested in tracking general categories of the buyers of my books, I record the dollar value (k) of books sold in state for resale, (l) state tax-exempt purchases, (m) in-state individual purchases, (n) books sold out of state for resale, to (o) out-of-state tax-exempt purchases, and (p) out-of-state individual purchases. Each of these columns (number of books sold, sales tax, total price, total paid, and all the buyer columns) are totaled. Again, make a Summary Table showing the sums of the buyer columns. The sum of the buyer columns should agree with the sum of the column of the total price of the book listed in the General Cash Ledger. Make considerable effort to keep these two reconciled. A little carelessness can wreak havoc on your time. For this sort of tracking, I have used a simple spreadsheet such as with Microsoft excel.

General Sales Ledger Headings

I also set a Summary Table tracking the number of books sold each month. In this manner, I watch for patterns of activity, and am able to make predictions about additional sales activity. I also list the date and recipient of any review copies issued in a subset of this spreadsheet. With some spreadsheets (such as Microsoft EXCEL), you can link data from one spreadsheet to another. This table makes it easy to generate regular reports, as you can simply calculate the difference in items from one month to the next.

Specific Accounts Sheets

Specific Accounts tracks orders and payments from buyers. These records provide the information on accounts outstanding. It is useful to set up individual ledgers for buyers, especially those who appear to be repeat buyers. On these ledgers, record the date and size of purchase (this is the same information as in the General Book Sale Sheet), plus purchase order number, if any. You may find it simplest to keep a single ledger ("Singles") for the numerous purchases that will probably not be repeat purchases. Keep a Summary Sheet which maintains running information on Accounts.

Total Book Orders	**$8,495.81**
Total State sales	**$5,627.95**
Total non-State sales	**$2,237.62**
Total paid sales	**$7,865.58**

Sales Tax Summary Table

Inventory Tracking Sheet

Maintain a count of the number of books (Inventory) you have on hand on a monthly basis on the Inventory Tracking Sheet. Your books—your stock in trade—are your assets. The number (and value) must be reported when tax reporting time comes around. The rate at which you move them out dictates when to order another press run. Your starting inventory is the number of saleable copies you get from the printer. When they arrive, note how many are packed in a box and note both the number of books *and* the number of boxes. The number of books on hand divided by the number per box will give a count of boxes on hand, which is useful for checking inventory.

If you maintain your Book Sales ledger properly, you will have a current count of the number of books sold. If at the same time, you maintain a current listing of review copies out, it should be a simple matter to determine the number of books on hand. Again, with an Inventory Tracking sheet, a month-by-month list of books sold gives you a sense of buying patterns. It is also quite satisfying to maintain a cumulative (year-by-year) total of books sold.

Database Records

A database is essentially a list, a collection of information you can manipulate. The most common *type* of list you will use is a mailing list. With a database program, you can organize and extract information as you desire.

In setting up your database, decide what information you want. Naturally, the most basic information is Contact person, Publication (or organization), Street Address or Post Office Box, City, State or Province, and ZIP code. You may wish to add a comment field. Devise some sort of coding system so that you can elicit as detailed and precise information as you may want.

Keep a database of your buyers. This is different from the spreadsheet records just described, since here you describe the buyer more fully. That is, include the Buyer's name, address, and descriptive notations such as the apparent source of purchase. A database is much easier to extract sorted information from than is a spreadsheet (at least, in my experience). In setting up the Buyers file, for instance, you may have your bookstore, school library, public library and individual buyers as well as the wholesalers and distributors who order. By coding these different buyers, you can detect trends of sales just as you can with geographical data. Geographical data on orders can be enlightening, and enables you to plot your marketing efforts more effectively.

Paperwork Forms Necessary for Fulfillment

Fulfillment—the shipping of books that have been ordered—requires a certain amount of paperwork. If you have an impact printer (a dot-matrix or a daisy wheel printer), the following forms are useful to have set up as template files on your computer. If you understand building and using macros, use them. Standard, basic forms such as a mailing label, a packing invoice, a billing invoice or the UPS counter records, can use an inordinate amount of time if you have to redo the setup for it each time (as you would with a typewriter). Set up templates that consistently use the same information (book name, ISBN, unit price, etc.) so that all you have to do is change the pertinent information for any given transaction. The guiding principle should be to get everything done with a minimum of effort.

Glossary

BACK MATTER. Appended material, such as a references section, glossary, bibliography, index, etc.

BACKLIST. Books published more than a few years ago that sell without being actively promoted.

BAR CODE. The symbol placed on the back of the book, capable of being read by an optical scanner, to provide a specific set of information about the item bearing the code.

BINDING. The means of holding the signatures of a book together. Bindings may be glue (perfect or a hybrid process such as Otabind or Rep-Kover) or a mechanical means such as wire, plastic comb (PVC), or ring binder (notebook).

BROCHURE. A piece of printed material used to describe a book, event, or other item. Customarily it has more than one page (sheet).

CAMERA-READY. The term used to describe material prepared for "shooting." Much printing now is done by the photo-offset process, which uses a big camera for producing film used for the printing plates.

CASE, CASE BINDING, CASE BOUND. Case (or properly, cased) binding is used with sewn signatures in cloth binding.

CLOTH, CLOTH BINDING, CLOTHBOUND. One type of binding for hardcover books. (Leather or other material is sometimes used to cover books as well. The signatures in some clothbound books are actually stitched (Smythe sewn) together before the binding is applied.

CORPORATION. A type of business organization in which the business becomes a legal entity.

COVER. A book's outside skin. Book covers are classed as "hard" or "soft." The type of cover affects the kind of binding used.

DATABASE. A collection of information that can be organized and sorted to extract specific material. A telephone directory is an example of material extracted from phone service orders placed with a phone company. Such a directory doesn't need to include the date an individual became a customer, or the type of service ordered, or any other information elicited at the initiation of service. A database program enables a user to collect and organize information.

DESKTOP PUBLISHING. The capability of producing camera-ready copy for publications (flyers, newsletters, etc.) by means of personal computer, appropriate computer programs (software) and printer. The term "desktop" implies, with considerable accuracy, that much or all of the work of producing a publication could be done by a single person in a single office with two pieces of physical equipment (computer and printer) that sit on a desk or tabletop.

DIRECT MAIL. The shortened term for direct mail marketing, where sales materials aim directly at the prospective end user, or individual book buyer.

DIRECT MARKETING. Marketing done directly to the prospective end user, or individual book buyer, usually in mail solicitations. The seller bypasses wholesalers and distributors. Direct marketing targets highly specific groups, and thus requires carefully-built mailing lists.

DISTRIBUTOR. A middle point between the publisher and booksellers. The distinction between a distributor and a wholesaler sometimes tends to blur. Generally speaking, a distributor carries a smaller number of titles than does the wholesaler and commonly produces a catalog used by its sales force which works directly with book buyers for stores.

DOUBLE WIRE BINDING. A type of mechanical binding using wire shaped into double wire loops going through perforations in the paper. Its advantage over spiral binding is its greater durability.

FACE. See TYPEFACE.

FLYER. A single sheet of material usually printed front and back for descriptive (advertising) purposes.

FONT. A given typeface in a particular size.

FRONT MATTER. All the pages up to the beginning of the text proper. Included are the half-title page; the verso (back) of the half-title page; the title page; on the verso of the title page is the copyright page; the dedication, if any; and the Table of Contents.

FRONTLIST. The newly-produced publications of a publisher.

GALLEY. A copy of a book's page layouts. Reviewers expecting galleys do not expect to see illustrations that might be in the book. Copies of camera-ready copy may be comb-bound (PVC) or a version that is essentially a replica of the finished book. Costs run about $10 per copy.

HARD COVER. The cover of a book that is heavier and more rigid than the light card stock used for soft cover books. The cover will extend slightly beyond the cut edges of the text pages, whereas soft cover books have cover and text pages cut flush. Various materials are used, and a paper wrapper, or dust jacket, may also be used to protect the cover.

ISBN. Stands for International Standard Book Number. The ISBN is to a book what your social security number is to you. Every book, every form (paper or cloth) of a book, every edition has its own ISBN that serves as its identifier. Hyphens are important: the four divisions of an ISBN identify the language of the book, the publisher, and the title itself. The fourth digit is a check number linked with the third group.

KEYLINES, KEYLINED TEXT, KEYLINING. The intermediate stage between typesetter and printer. Printed text and graphics are placed on page forms, ready for printing. Formerly, the typesetter prepared copy—sections of printed copy and illustrations—printed in long strips that were then cut and pasted in place on boards that were photographed (photo-offset) for printing production. Desktop page layout programs have essentially eliminated this stage.

MASS MARKET. A very large general market or audience. Titles for the mass market are expected to sell in great quantities (press runs in the tens and hundreds of thousands) quickly.

MECHANICAL BINDING. Bindings using wire, staples or plastic.

MIDLIST. A title that has been out some time. Previous books by an author and which may or may not be still in print are midlist titles.

MULTIPLE SALES. See SALES, MULTIPLE.

OTABIND™. A binding process for trade paperbacks that resembles perfect binding (it has a printable spine) but allows a book to be opened out flat.

OUT-OF-PRINT. Publishers declare books out-of-print generally when they have run out of stock of the title.

PAGE-LAYOUT PROGRAM. A computer program enabling a designer to plan the layout of the pages of a flyer, brochure, or whatever.

The designer can add and manipulate graphic elements as well as text.

PARTNERSHIP, LIMITED. Type of business structure. A partnership in which the limited partners share in the partnership's liability only up to the amount of their investment in the limited partnership.

PERFECT BINDING. A common binding for paperback books. Glue applied to the trimmed spines of the signatures holds the cover to the book. This is generally the least expensive means of binding a book of half-inch or greater thickness.

PREPRESS SERVICE BUREAU. Shop specializing in preparing computer data for printing. A service bureau can also optically scan non-textual material such as photographs or art work, translating them into computer code for reproduction in a publication. Usually a bureau can then produce camera-ready work.

PREPRODUCTION EXPENSES. Expenses incurred before a book is produced. Generally this includes research, manuscript preparation (e.g., typing), editing, acquiring desired illustrations, et cetera. Some include cover design expenses here, rather than in actual production expenses.

PRESS RELEASE. The piece sent to the media ("press") announcing an event. It answers the traditional five "Ws"—who, what, where, when, and why, and perhaps how. The proper form includes the name of a contact person and phone number and a stated release time (For Immediate Release; To Be Released after *x date*). This calls for journalistic writing, where the most important items come first. The text should be double-spaced.

PRINT RUN. Number of copies to be printed ordered.

PRODUCTION EXPENSES. Expenses of production generally include typesetting, keylining (if necessary), printing and binding.

PROMOTION. As used in publishing, the root sense of this word, the "moving forward," describes the activity of making people favorably aware of a book.

RFQ. Request for quotation or bid. An RFQ is the list of specifications of desired items that is sent to a prospective vendor. The vendor in turn replies with a bid, the price(s) that would be charged for the job.

SALES, MULTIPLE. Sale of multiple copies of the book.

SALES, REPEAT. Recurring sales; often the buyers are bookstores, wholesalers or distributors.

SALES, SINGLE. Sale of one copy of the book. Small publishers often call such orders "onesies" or "twosies."

SERVICE BUREAU. See PREPRESS SERVICE BUREAU

SIGNATURE. A unit of counting pages for determining book size. A signature contain 8, 16 or 32 pages of the printed book. Many book printers use sheet-fed presses, that is, presses that print one large sheet at a time. The count comes from folding a sheet twice, three or four times, and trimming the edges. For printing, the printer places each keylined page in position so that when printed, folded and trimmed, pages are in proper order. For insight into the operation, fold a sheet of paper in half, and repeat the process. This gives you an 8-page signature. Mark each section as it would read in a finished book. Make sure you indicate which edge is at the top. When you have done this, open out the sheet to see where and how each page lies; note that both sides of the sheet are printed on.

SINGLE SALES. See SALES, SINGLE.

SOFT COVER. Refers to paperbound books with nonrigid covers. Bindings may be perfect, Otabind, or mechanical bindings using wire or plastic. See also Hard Cover.

SOLE PROPRIETORSHIP. Single ownership. You (as the sole proprietor) can put money into the company and take it out as desired. Proprietor is responsible for reporting profits or sales taxes to the federal and state tax offices.

SPECIFICATION SHEET. The instructions for the type font and size for text, captions, headings, etc., and placement of captions and illustrations given to the typesetter.

SPREADSHEET. Term used for computer programs for manipulating numbers. It consists of a matrix of rows and columns. The intersection of a single row and column is called a cell. Information and instructions for calculations can be entered in cells.

STYLE SHEET. Term used in desktop publishing and typesetting for the listing of the different styles used in a publication. For example, in the preparation of this book, all chapter headings (name and number of chapter) were identified, with a name and definition of what was to be used for all such headings. The Recommended Reading involved several styles (e.g., the listing of the data about each book cited; the comments made about the book and the subheadings) to insure a consistency of appearance. In page layout programs, a change in a style sheet definition is enacted immediately throughout the publication. My computer has a color monitor, and I used color as a part of each style's definition when working on each section to insure every line, every sentence was properly defined with a desired style.

STYLEBOOK. Also called a handbook of style. A book such as the *Chicago Manual of Style,* where a publisher describes and illustrates the preferred way of handling all matters pertaining to the content of a book. The purpose of a stylebook is to insure consistency and correct handling. Desk dictionaries may contain a basic handbook of style.

TRADE PAPERBACK. Books in paper covers that are expected to have a longer life and meet more specialized interests; they are "quality" books.

TYPEFACE. Face or typeface refers to the *style* of the letter or the character of the type, in short, what it looks like.

WHOLESALER. A book buyer between the publisher and the bookseller. The wholesaler buys large numbers of titles for the buyer to choose from. Distributors may buy from wholesalers.

WIRE-O BINDING. A trade name. See DOUBLE WIRE BINDING.

Index

(Compiled by Eileen Quam and Theresa Wolner)

About the Author

Patricia J. Bell is the president-owner of Cat's-paw Press, a company she formed in 1986 to publish her first book, *Roughing It Elegantly: A Practical Guide to Canoe Camping. The Paddler's Planner*, followed. The *Prepublishing Handbook: What you should know* before *you publish your first book* is her latest.

She holds degrees in education and English from the University of Oklahoma. An early major in journalism fostered a persisting interest in publishing. She has taught Latin and language arts.

A member of the Minnesota (now Midwest) Independent Publishers Association (MIPA) since 1986, she has served as vice-president, Membership Chairperson and Vice-president for Outreach. In 1992, she became MIPA's first Executive Secretary and she was the recipient of MIPA's first Landmark Award for distinguished service to the book publishing industry.

In 1989, she was a partner in establishing Tessera Publishing, Inc., and is the company's managing editor.

Well-known in her area small press community, she often speaks to groups on self-, or independen, publishing. She teaches classes on the financial and temporal logistics of independent publication.

Prior to becoming a publisher, Pat, an active member of the Minnesota Solar Energy Association (now the Minnesota Renewable Energy Society) was the founder-editor of its Newsletter, the latest in a series of newsletters she has produced.

Pat and husband Don, residents of Eden Prairie, Minnesota since 1968, have four grown children.

Her interests include classical music, gardening, natural history, and canoe-camping.

ORDER FORM

9561 Woodridge Circle
Eden Prairie, Minnesota 55347

Please send me ______ copy (copies) of **The *Prepublishing Handbook*: What you should *know* before you publish your first book,** by Patricia J. Bell. I am enclosing $12 (plus $0.78 sales tax, if in Minnesota) and $1.50 for shipping for each copy.

Please send me ______ copy (copies) of **The Paddler's Planner.** I am enclosing $7.95 (plus $.52 sales tax, if in Minnesota) and $1.50 for shipping for each copy.

Please send me ______ copy (copies) of **Roughing It Elegantly: A Practical Guide To Canoe Camping**, by Patricia J. Bell (revised edition). I am enclosing $11.95 (plus $0.78 sales tax, if in Minnesota) and $1.50 for shipping for each copy.

Name ____

Address ______________________________________

____

_____ Yes, I would like the above book(s) autographed to:

____

____

____

ALSO FROM CAT'S-PAW PRESS

Roughing It Elegantly: A Practical Guide To Canoe Camping

by Patricia J. Bell

Enjoy North America's finest canoe wilderness elegantly—simply, efficiently, and with style.

What they said about the first edition (judged a Classic Merit winner, Midwest Book Awards)...

"Pleasant, encouraging, environmentally-conscious,...a sensible, personal discussion of canoe camping." **Library Journal**

"An excellent resource and reference book." Minneapolis **Star Tribune**

"Offers the perspective of the ordinary camper who is also a woman." Eden Prairie (Minnesota) **Sailor**

"The sort of book a guy gets for his woman if he wants her to go canoeing with him." St. Paul (Minnesota) **Pioneer Press**

"Even beginners will feel at ease by following her well-explained, clear directions." Woodstock **Vermont Standard**

"Offers a wealth of practical tips and information...a valuable handguide for both experienced and not-so-experienced campers." Duluth (Minnesota) **News-Tribune**

"Outstanding guide to canoe camping...stylishly written...should appeal to all outdoor types." St. Cloud (Minnesota) **Daily Times**

"I could have used all the wonderful advice of ***Roughing It Elegantly*** when I first took to the woods...my husband could have used the book, too." **Minnesota Reviews**

"Shows how anyone can safely and comfortably enjoy a wilderness experience." Greg Leis, Executive Director, **Wilderness Inquiry**

ISBN- 0-9618227-0-8 $11.95 USA 160 pp.

The Paddler's Planner by Patricia J. Bell

It's easier for the camper to rough it elegantly — efficiently, simply and with his or her own style — with ***The Paddler's Planner.***

It's a planner!

- Plan nine upcoming trips using the **Master Check Lists** .
- Read **Food Suggestions** for wilderness trips.

It's a log!

- Record 75 trip days in your **Trip Log**.
- Record equipment purchases, dates and their costs in **Our Equipment List**.
- Note down **Addresses** of contacts for permits, reservations , information.
- Use **Reminders** to note items to clean, repair, return, replace or acquire.
- Make **Notes** for additional comments or reminders.

ISBN 0-9618227-3-2 $7.95 USA 200 pp